Wave-

Rings

in the

Water

CARMEN JOHNSON

Wave-Rings in the Water

My Years with the

Women of Postwar Japan

With a Foreword by
Yuka Moriguchi Tsuchiya,
Hiroshima University

CHARLES RIVER PRESS   ALEXANDRIA, VIRGINIA

Published by

CHARLES RIVER PRESS

427 Old Town Court

Alexandria, VA 22314-3544.

Design by Bonnie Campbell.

Map by Alex Tait, Equator Graphics.

Cover photograph: © The Stock Market/Marvy!

Photographs in insert used with the permission of
Carmen Johnson.

Library of Congress Cataloging-in-Publication Data

Johnson, Carmen, 1910–

    Wave-rings in the water : my years with the women
of postwar Japan / Carmen Johnson.

      p.   cm.

    Includes bibliographical references and index.

    ISBN 0-9647124-1-5 (pbk.)

    1. Japan—History—Allied occupation, 1945–
1952—Personal narratives. 2. Johnson, Carmen,
1910– . 3. Women—Japan—social conditions.
I. Title.

    DS889.16.J65

952.04'4'082—dc20   96-11798

                              CIP

Printed on recycled paper

Manufactured in the United States of America

10 9 8 7 6 5 4 3 2 1

Contents • • •

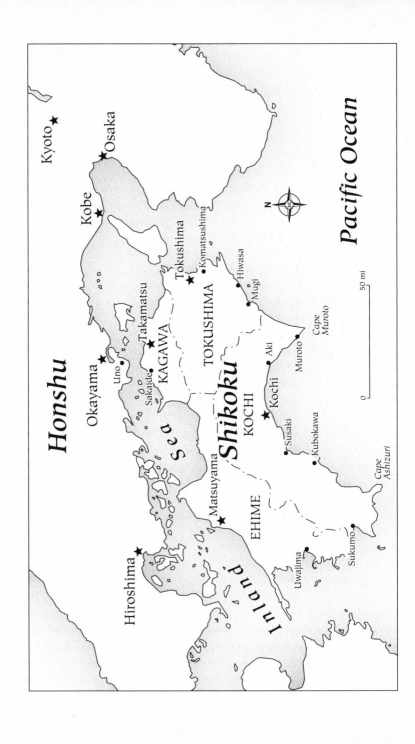

Foreword

Military occupation of a defeated country and women's groups—there may seem to be scarcely any link between these two subjects. Readers may be surprised, however, to learn that all kinds of democratic women's groups and even Girl Scouts were nurtured in occupied Japan immediately after World War II by American women occupation officers. This book presents the exciting firsthand experience of one of those women.

Two important objectives of the occupation of Japan were demilitarization and democratization. To democratize Japanese society and to destroy the roots of militarism and ultranationalism, the Americans thought that not only the laws but also the thoughts and customs deep-rooted in the everyday life of the Japanese people had to be changed.

One of those obnoxious customs was gender discrimination. There were all kinds of institutional and moral discrimination against women in prewar Japan. Confucian morals taught women to be always obedient to their fathers, brothers, and husbands, and chastity was emphasized as the utmost feminine virtue. However, those customs were not necessarily the comprehensive tradition of Japanese history. In fact, before the dawning of modern times, strict Confucian moral values were mostly observed by the ruling *samurai* class; such values were quite alien to the families of merchants, peasants, and fishermen.

After the Meiji Restoration (1868), however, Japan undertook rapid modernization and industrialization, and political leaders sought a strong ideological basis for establishing national unity. For this purpose, Confucian morality was advocated and infused into the population at large through education. While there were many public girls' schools, their major purpose was mass-producing "good wives and wise mothers" to serve the new working-class men who were expected to contribute to the government-led modernization.

The end result of these government policies included all-male universities; the Family Code, which treated women as "legal incompetents"; and the Criminal Code, which punished only women, not men, for adultery. In the private sphere, people came to think it natural to place wives second to husbands, and daughters second to sons.

Even before World War II, there were some brave women— teachers, suffragists, and leftist writers—who tried to bring about changes in this situation. Their efforts led the Japanese government to grudgingly improve education for women and at least to "consider" allowing female suffrage. However, no radical changes occurred—not until Japan was defeated and occupied by the Allied forces.

After the war, all the laws that discriminated by race, creed, sex, social status, or family origin were repealed or reformed by the Japanese government under the guidance of American specialists working with General MacArthur's GHQ (General Headquarters). The new legal and educational systems in postwar Japan guaranteed Japanese women equal rights on paper.

However, this was the most the occupation authorities first intended to do. There were only vague, rather confused ideas about women's rights in the original policies. General MacArthur

and other top-ranking occupation officers knew that female suffrage was an indispensable part of democracy; however, he
described its purpose as making the government "subservient to
the well being of the home," not as strengthening women's rights
per se. When a female American member of the drafting committee for the new Japanese constitution proposed that concrete
stipulations on women's rights be included, higher-ranking officers disagreed. With the even more fierce objections raised by
some male Japanese politicians, in the end only the most basic
part of the equal rights article remained in the constitution.

In fact, while most occupation authorities regarded Japanese
women as war victims who needed help, they were not particularly enthusiastic about women's rights. However, American
women in the occupation—both in the central and local organizations—played an important role in making occupation policies
concerning women's rights real and concrete rather than abstract.
They carried out much more detailed and radical plans to enhance
women's status than the top-ranking officers had in mind.

In CI&E (the Civil Information and Education section), one
of the Special Staff Sections of GHQ, there was a position called
"women's information officer." WAC Lieutenant Ethel Weed was
appointed to this position, and she and her colleagues planned to
appoint twenty-seven American women as "women's affairs officers" to work with local military government teams all over the
country. These women were expected to educate Japanese
women concerning their new rights and principles of democracy. The author of the present book, former WAC Lieutenant
Carmen Johnson, was appointed as women's affairs officer in
charge of all four prefectures of Shikoku Island, the smallest of
the four main islands of Japan.

What Johnson tried to do, in essence, was to help people
internalize and put into practice the principles of democracy.
Her testimony shows how democratic reforms were carried out
at the grassroots with the guidance and cooperation of an Ameri-

can woman officer. As a Japanese woman and a scholar of history, I find her writing extremely attractive both as a historical document and as an autobiographical essay of an American woman engaged in this important work.

To many Japanese women who lived in the countryside, Johnson offered the first opportunity to learn about democratic procedures and women's rights. Perhaps they had already learned by newspaper or radio or at school that democracy and equal rights were guaranteed by the new constitution. But Johnson's simple and concrete explanations probably had much greater impact than the media announcements. Her achievements can also be attributed to her personality. She talked to Japanese women as a peer working with them to achieve their goals, without the arrogance of the occupier. As a consequence, many women, particularly those who were eager to improve women's status and construct a new democratic society, accepted her both as a friend and a mentor.

Johnson's first book was published in Japan in 1986 as *Senryo Nikki: Kusanone no Onnatachi*. It was through this book that I came to know her when I was a graduate student of history in the United States. As I was working on my research on Family Law reform during the Allied occupation, I became very interested in her firsthand testimony on how the egalitarian principles of the new law were explained to the Japanese people at the grassroots. I interviewed her and was instantly attracted by her frank and warm personality. Such episodes in the book as when she declined gifts and meals offered by Japanese people because she did not want to "eat food that was scarce and have it subsidized by money intended for education" typify her conscientiousness.

It is extremely meaningful for her story to be published in the original English language (and with richer contents than in the earlier Japanese edition) on the fiftieth anniversary of her departure for Japan. I strongly hope that many American people, particularly those interested in women's history and U.S.–Japan relations, will read this heartwarming inside story of the Allied occupation.

It may be hard to conclude simply whether Johnson's work was successful; sometimes it was very successful, and sometimes it was not. Her lectures and discussion sessions might not have brought about immediate changes in gender discrimination. And there were things simply beyond her power to affect, even though she tried, particularly when the central government was involved. However, the following example tells us what it meant to have her in one local community. In a students' English speech contest in which she was one of the judges, one boy and one girl tied for first place. A Japanese judge (possibly a teacher) suggested the boy be given the first, just because he was male. However, Johnson and her boss declared that was unfair, and finally convinced the Japanese judges to award two firsts. She recollects, "I think such a dilemma probably would never have occurred under usual Japanese procedures at the time. The judges would privately have reached a consensus and declared the boy the winner."

Although this kind of change was small, it had important implications. Questions were raised about the way things had been done before, and more importantly, there were people (especially women) who welcomed the question-raising with applause. And I like to think that the young female student went on to greater accomplishments in her life, her self-confidence boosted by the prize—though never knowing about the gutsy American woman whose intervention was key to the decision-making.

The fact that Johnson herself was in many ways a pioneer professional woman explains why she could truly sympathize with Japanese women who pioneered into various occupations and fields, such as local elected officials, social reformers, Girl Scout leaders. To them, Johnson was a role model, providing an example they could not find among Japanese women in small towns.

In today's Japan, what Johnson calls "the conflict between past and future" is still alive. In spite of improved educational and job opportunities, women are still sparse in decision-making positions. The 1995 United Nations Development Program report on 160 nations showed that Japan ranks third in terms of income and education levels. However, when it comes to women's participation in political and business decision-making, Japan's rank goes down to twenty-seventh. Japanese women hold only 2.4 percent (twelve seats) of the Lower House seats of the Diet and 3.5 percent of the seats in prefectural, city, town, and village assemblies around the country.

However, the situation keeps evolving. For instance, 36.8 percent of women now receive higher education, and more and more of them are pioneering into professional and decision-making positions. The notion that women should stay at home and men go out as breadwinners still remains, but now that more than half of all married women are employed, such a notion is also changing.

The reforms during the occupation may not have wielded direct influence on these changes in later years. However, Johnson and other American women officers certainly threw small stones to start the "wave-rings in the water." Cooperation between American and Japanese women under the military occupation reminds us what global sisterhood can do to better the world.

—Yuka Moriguchi Tsuchiya
Research Associate & Lecturer
Hiroshima University

1 · · ·

A Ginkgo

Tree in

the Distance

Japan's surrender to the Allies in August 1945 was momentous not only for the unprecedented period of war it ended but for the remarkable period of peace it began. At the end of World War II, Japan's cities, industry, and agriculture lay in ruins, its people devastated both physically and emotionally. Under the direction of Japan's military leaders, virtually every aspect of the people's lives had been marshaled toward conquest and war for the past decade and a half. Now, their way of life and system of beliefs defeated, their leaders dead or on trial for war crimes, they were confused, hungry, and willing to cooperate with their occupiers. At this critical moment in world history, the victorious Allied forces—led by the United States—determined to reform Japan so that militarism would never rule there again. Under the direction of General Douglas MacArthur, a man controversial in many ways but well suited for this job, Americans went to Japan to launch the massive and radical project of changing Japan from an authoritarian, ultranationalist country to a land of democracy and equal rights.

As Edwin O. Reischauer said in *Japan: The Story of a Nation*, "Never before had one advanced nation attempted to reform from within the supposed faults of another advanced nation. And never did the military occupation of one world power by another prove so satisfactory to the victors and so tolerable to the vanquished."

What Reischauer put in national terms I can attest to on a personal level, for I was a member of the occupation force, spending one year in Nagoya, a large city 180 miles southwest of Tokyo, and then three and a half years on Shikoku, the smallest of Japan's four main islands. My job for most of that period was teaching democratic practices and equal rights to Japanese women at the grassroots. For me, the primary reward of those years is the satisfaction of having helped bring about changes for Japanese women. However, the experience changed me as well, for I learned lessons, developed interests, and made friendships that have enriched my life for the past fifty years.

In many ways, my journey to Japan grew out of attitudes and expertise developed throughout my youth and young adulthood, never suspecting that they would be of later use in such an exotic locale. I was born May 9, 1910, in Elkhorn, Wisconsin (population 2,000). My parents of Swedish ancestry named me after Carmen Sylva, then queen of Romania, hoping that an unusual first name would counter the relative ordinariness of our family name.

Although my high school, like many others at the time, had no guidance or counseling services, I knew that I wanted to go to college. I also knew that professions for women were generally limited to teaching and librarianship. When, a few days before I graduated from high school, my outgoing, good-natured father died—only hours after selling his dry-goods store—my career was decided for me. With my older brother working his way through the University of Wisconsin, my mother accepted my father's eldest sister's offer to let me live with her in DeKalb, Illinois, and attend Northern Illinois State Teachers College. When that aunt died suddenly of cancer, another aunt—my mother's sister—who lived nearby took me in, and I graduated with the two-year degree then required to teach elementary school.

The next five years teaching in Kewanee, Illinois, during the Depression were rough. Early on, I lost my little savings when our bank failed. My beginning salary of $100 a month for nine months in 1929 was gradually cut to $70 by 1934. During that time, half of my earnings were paid in cash and half in notes to be redeemed later. Rice, the most affordable food, was my mealtime staple; I ate so much of it then that for years afterwards I couldn't swallow it at all.

In spite of the difficulties, I remember those years as a time of professional growth, good friendships, and genuine fun. A young, enthusiastic executive for the Girl Scouts brought together seven or eight of us new teachers to become troop leaders. In addition to that volunteer work during school months, I was a counselor at Girl Scout camps in the summers. Then, in 1936, after I had earned a bachelor of education degree, the Girl Scouts in Oak Park, Illinois, offered me a professional position, visiting troops in the area and training leaders. I was still in that position when the United States entered the war in 1941.

The Army's public relations efforts certainly succeeded with me! Like so many other young people at the time, I was patriotic and believed that my country needed me, especially because announcements emphasized that women could replace men for active duty. So I volunteered for the Women's Army Auxiliary Corps (WAAC), which on July 1, 1943, became the Women's Army Corps (WAC). Much later I learned that an eye doctor who examined me during an early physical recommended that I be given a certificate of disability because of my poor eyesight. For reasons unknown, that recommendation for discharge was never processed.

I had basic training in Daytona Beach, Florida, followed by Officer Candidate School in Des Moines, Iowa. My initial temporary duty was at a fort connected with the Air Force at Sault Sainte Marie, Michigan, where carriers of iron ore for the war effort passed through the locks of the Soo Canals. I found that I quite liked my job there as an officer working with radar warnings. After that, I was sent to California, where for the rest of the war I held watch positions in combat intelligence with the Fourth Air Force in San Diego, Oakland, and San Francisco. The most exciting of these postings was the last, in San Francisco, for during that time the Japanese sent across the Pacific free-floating balloons of oiled paper, carrying incendiary bombs to start fires (especially in forests) or personnel bombs to kill. In an attempt to confuse the Japanese, the Office of Censorship asked that news editors and radio announcers not report any sightings or recoveries of the balloons. All complied with this request until six people were killed on a picnic in Oregon on May 5, 1945. According to my records, we ended up with a total count of 285 balloons.

Another part of my job in San Francisco was to organize and declassify military documents and photographs, mostly aerial shots, of Japan. This job fascinated me, for like most Americans at the time, I knew very little about that country. Of course, I'd heard the propaganda and seen racist caricatures, but I didn't believe the Japanese people were really like that. As my interest grew, I began to read everything I could get my hands on about Japan. I loved the names of cities there and often repeated them to myself just for the sounds: Sendai, Nagoya, Sapporo, Kyoto, Osaka.

With the war's end in 1945, I had decisions to make. I knew I didn't want to return to the Girl Scouts. In fact, I didn't want to settle down yet—the taste of adventure I'd gained in the war years only whetted my appetite for more. Somehow I had heard of the Allied military government being set up in Japan as the link between General MacArthur, the Supreme Commander for the Allied Powers (SCAP, pronounced "scap"), and Japanese officials and citizens at the local and prefectural levels. There were two roughly parallel structures. On the Allied side, MacArthur's headquarters staff (also referred to as SCAP) made policy decisions and sent directives down to military governments in the prefectures (political divisions similar to U.S. states). On the Japanese side, the same directives moved downward from Japanese ministries to local governments. Men and women of the military government—mostly Americans—would be responsible for working with the Japanese people to implement SCAP directives and the provisions of the new democratic constitution, which would go into effect in 1947.

Well, I needed a job, I was familiar with the military, I knew that I could adapt to various living conditions, I'd been a teacher, and I had a great interest in Japan. The situation seemed just right for me, so after being demobilized, I headed for Washington, D.C., in search of a civilian job with the occupation—something, I hoped, that would take advantage of my background. Alas, my dreams exceeded reality, for although I visited a number of offices, nobody offered me a job. Finally, I accepted a job as a clerk-typist with the Fifth Air Force in Nagoya—fearing that the office work would be boring, but happy that this assignment would at least get me to Japan.

In the literal sense, my journey to Japan began near midnight on July 5, 1946, when I boarded the tourist Pullman in Chicago. After two days and three nights crossing the continent by train and nearly three weeks in Seattle while the ship was readied for the Pacific crossing, we finally embarked on July 26. The ship's name, *Sea Star,* conjured up images of starlit nights with cool breezes and romantic encounters. In reality, the *Sea Star* was a converted cargo ship with bare accommodations. The women in our group—employees of the U.S. government, the Red Cross, and the USO—were the only passengers we saw, but we were told that hundreds of soldiers were quartered below. We women clambered up and down a steep metal ladder between the living quarters and the deck, slept on triple-decker steel cots, showered without privacy, and used a toilet where some ten bare adjoining seats backed up to ten more. For a few nights we shivered with cold, before a southerly route left us perspiring in our cots with no air moving.

The monotony of fourteen days at sea was broken somewhat by unexpected events. We were thrilled by our first glimpse of flying fish on the fifth day out and a little uneasy that same day when an albatross followed us, not able to remember exactly what had happened between another such bird and Coleridge's ancient mariner. Two whales appeared far in the distance, and on the last day at sea, a school of perhaps a hundred porpoises put on a show quite close to the ship.

Evenings spent on the fantail were the best time of all. First were the sunsets. Then, as the light faded, phosphorescence began to glow along the sides of the ship as it slipped through the water. We spent hours in the dark leaning on the rail and watching the light dim and sharpen. The moon, rather new as we left Seattle, fattened as we sailed, leaving a trail of silver on the ocean. Last of all came the stars—big and bright—that rocked gently in the sky to the motion of the ship.

Early on the morning of August 9, small Japanese islands began to appear. After breakfast, we went on deck, excited by our first views of Japan. We all recognized as Mount Fuji the cone-shaped mountain that appeared and disappeared in the clouds along the horizon. And for the first time since leaving Seattle, we saw ships. As we entered Tokyo Bay, the color of the water turned from a beautiful blue to a dark green. Jellyfish, barely visible in the bay's depths, resembled raw eggs with white yolks.

After docking in Yokohama, we were loaded onto buses for Tokyo and told that our luggage would follow. Although I knew that both cities had been half destroyed during the war, I was stunned by my first view of the devastation. Our bus made its way through long stretches of bombed-out areas, containing only hovels made of scraps. Hurrying people tried to board crowded streetcars, most of the men dressed in bits of military uniforms, many carrying knapsacks. We laughed only once—when we saw a sign advertising in English, "Speedily—Carefully—Laundry."

We women assigned to the Fifth Air Force were deposited— still without our luggage—at the four-story Army Hall, formerly used by Japanese army officers, located near Tokyo's Imperial Palace. A young Japanese man, speaking excellent English with a British accent, greeted us and assigned us rooms. When the crowd learned that the rooms contained neither soap nor towels, many complained most impolitely. He disappeared briefly, then returned with a few towels and bars of soap—his personal belongings. My new roommate, Mary Hopkins, and I came away with half a bar of soap.

Our room on the fourth floor overlooked the Empress Moat, whose green-terraced grassy bank ended at a high stone wall. We reviewed our resources and decided to use our slips for night-clothes and the pillowcases as towels. After washing in the lavatory, we proceeded to the dining room, a spacious, attractive area with table linens and an orchestra. While waiting to be served, we overheard an American woman at the next table talking to the Japanese waitress about her meal. "No mashed potatoes," she announced firmly in English, adding, we assumed, the same request in Japanese. Mary and I, impressed, looked at each other in anticipation that someday we too might be able to order meals like that. When the dinner arrived at the neighboring table, however, not only was there a generous serving of mashed potatoes on the plate, but an extra dish of potatoes was served on the side.

Back in our room, a cricket on the sill of our unscreened window and a ginkgo tree in the distance reminded us that we would find familiar as well as unfamiliar sights in our new environment.

And there was the moon, now full, that had traveled with us across the ocean.

The next five days passed quickly, our luggage having arrived the day after we did. At an orientation, we learned that three thousand Allied civilians were now in Japan, with more than five thousand expected eventually. Our walks about the city included a visit to the Ginza with its sidewalk stands offering almost everything imaginable for sale. To see the Great Buddha and the Hachiman Shrine, we took a conducted trip to Kamakura by electric train in two special coaches. Although passengers were tightly packed on this and all other trains, through the windows we glimpsed the open countryside, lovely with the bright green of the growing rice set off by the soft brown of the farmhouses.

One evening, we went to the Imperial Theater for a Japanese performance of *Swan Lake* for members of the occupation. In the lobby, we saw the air conditioners: large pieces of ice standing in containers on the floor with a big electric fan behind each. The fourteen dancers seemed short and chubby in contrast to those in the United States, and all the men wore red wigs.

While in Tokyo, we also paid a brief visit to the War Ministry to observe the trials of Japanese wartime officials for war crimes. On a card given to each of us were the family names of the twenty-six defendants as they were seated, men neatly dressed in either civilian or undecorated military garb, some of them looking almost bored. General Tojo, however, formerly prime minister and army minister, was alert to the proceedings, had a briefcase beside him, and was taking notes.

During the time we spent in Tokyo, most of our interactions were with members of the occupation force; our only communication with Japanese citizens was brief encounters with maids and waitresses. Glimpses of people on the streets or on trains gave no idea of what life was really like for them one year after the end of the war.

What a lot I had to learn.

A Year

in Nagoya

arrived in Nagoya to begin my one-year appointment on August 16, 1946, after a nine-hour train ride from Tokyo. Along the way, with the ocean on the left, I saw fishing boats, terraced rice paddies, squat tea plants, farm men and women cultivating crops, and one automobile. Nearing Nagoya, we passed through the same kind of devastation we had seen when leaving Tokyo. Then, as we alighted from the train in the Nagoya station, for the first time I became aware of the wretched lot of hundreds—perhaps thousands—of homeless people. They were huddled on the floor of the station and crowded into passage-ways, holding close the bundles and knapsacks containing their few belongings. Even on a bright summer day, this shelter was damp, the odors fusty, the light dim. We did not need to be told why the station was off-limits for occupation personnel—it was home for these people.

Nagoya, formerly a large manufacturing center, had been 90 percent destroyed by bombings and fires—houses burned, stores and office buildings gutted, industrial plants wiped out. Block after block of rubble replaced what had once been homes. Only the foundations remained of historic Nagoya Castle, built in 1610 and used by the Japanese military during the war. One Sunday soon after my arrival I got a recreation jeep and driver to take me to the dock and factory areas. We drove for miles where nothing remained except ruins of buildings and pieces of machinery rusting in the grass.

The Fifth Air Force had confiscated the most usable of the few buildings left in the main business section for its headquarters, hospital, post exchange (PX), and billets for single military and civilian personnel. To provide dwellings for families of married officers, houses untouched by bombings were also attached. My group of women was housed in the Kanko Hotel for two weeks and then joined other civilian women when a refurbished office building was opened as the Chiyoda Hotel.

Most American civilians worked in the headquarters in the Yamato Building, a short walk from our hotels. There I was assigned to the Thirty-Fourth Statistical Control Unit of the Fifth Air Force as a clerk-typist, grade CAF-3. My annual salary of $2,377 included an overseas differential of 25 percent because Japan was considered a hardship post. (At that time, an excellent dinner in Seattle, complete with fingerbowl, cost $1.75.) In the beginning, as one of three women in the unit's administrative section, I was not busy. I spent my time typing personal letters; reading two daily newspapers—the *Nippon Times,* an English-language paper printed in Tokyo, and the military *Stars and Stripes*; and preparing class materials after I began helping Japanese businessmen and students improve their use of English. After some months, one woman and then the other left, and I became busy, promoted to a CAF-4, clerk, with an annual salary of $2,992, including differential.

Since hotels, headquarters, and PX were not far apart, much of our travel was on foot; but buses, jeeps, and trucks were used for longer trips. The six-by-six Army truck with a canvas roof and benches on the two long sides, familiarly referred to as a "six-by," was the usual mode of travel for group excursions.

Because I was heavy at the time, I experienced much difficulty in getting in and out of the back until some of the GIs and I became acquainted. Then, while some pushed and some pulled, we managed to get me in and out, though never in a manner that could be called graceful.

Because my job was clearly not going to provide many opportunities for interactions with Japanese people, I soon sought out my own connections. In this, I was unlike many Americans who remained in the cocoon placed around them by the occupation and limited themselves to American friends, entertainment, and shopping. Admittedly, SCAP encouraged this isolation by designating many places—banks, inns, hotels, theaters, schools, modes of travel, and restaurants—off-limits for security reasons. There were ways of getting around these regulations, however, by joining up with others in an authorized group or gaining special permission from the military police.

Thanks to opportunities available to civilian as well as military personnel, my travels were wide-ranging, and on thirty of the fifty-four weekends while I was assigned to Nagoya, I went on trips throughout the country. I soon found that the Japanese people were eager to become acquainted with Americans as individuals and not only as part of an occupation force. Japanese officials carefully planned for our comfort on these excursions. I noted in my journal that "police, chambers of commerce, the travel bureau, liaison officers with the railroads, assorted interpreters swarm[ed] all over the place. Any decisions made took a major conference." To the list should be added mayors, heads of businesses, entertainers, and railroad stationmasters. They always treated us with great courtesy and paid attention to even the smallest details. Whether we were more curious about the Japanese or they about us was an unanswered question.

On trips, also, I began to buy books about Japan: tourist handbooks at PXs; new books from gift shops in American installations, some of them translations from the Japanese; and used books, usually at secondhand bookstores that sold books from private Japanese libraries. I also ordered new and used books from catalogs of American bookstores.

As the weather turned cold, the Japanese people's lack of adequate clothing became apparent and all kinds of match-ups appeared; one of the strangest was high-buttoned shoes worn by a man. Because very few department stores had survived the bombings and yard goods were almost nonexistent, even those with money could not find clothes to purchase or fabric to make into clothing. One of the maids at our hotel reported with great anguish the theft of a neighbor's now-irreplaceable sewing machine. At five o'clock one morning early in November, we were awakened by the loud clattering of hundreds of wooden clogs, as people who had arrived on the first streetcar of the morning rushed past our hotel toward a department store that had advertised a sale of shoes.

The coming of winter also meant the onset of misery from the cold itself, for temperatures often fell below freezing. Charcoal was the fuel commonly used for cooking and heating, supplemented by small heaters when the intermittent electrical service was available. Before the war, people kept warm during the day by wearing layers of clothing, then fortified themselves for the cold night by taking hot baths and sleeping under several quilts. Because both fuel and clothing were now either scarce or nonexistent, most of those protections from the cold were unavailable.

The food shortage was severe. By accident one day, when I inadvertently interrupted the hotel maids at their lunch, I saw that each had only half of a large sweet potato for her meal. Because the people were hungry, many near starvation, the national government rationed food. In this country where rice was the staple food, I observed in my journal in June 1947 that "the Japanese are getting five days' ration a month of rice and the rest in other food." This other food—relief supplies from the

United States—included potatoes, wheat treated so that it could be cooked with rice, flour, dried fruit such as prunes and apricots, and beans. Signs on the streets exhorted people to eat the imported food, even though much of it was strange to them.

At the same time, black-market food prices skyrocketed as farmers found they could make more money selling their crops privately than through official government channels. The people of Nagoya, like those of other cities, regularly jammed the already crowded trains for the country to buy food on the black market or to barter a treasured kimono for vegetables. No aspect of the misery of the Japanese people touched me more than this struggle to the country to obtain food. On one cold winter day, traveling in a comfortable railroad coach for Americans, I looked across the platform and saw one for the Japanese: it had no glass in the windows, was unlighted and unheated, and yet was packed with people. Passengers entered and left the car through the windows more often than by the doors because of the mass of bodies packed inside.

"It all made me wonder how the Japanese people had courage to begin again" was the note in my journal. But they had. The streets were full of men and women going about their business, transported by streetcars that, like the trains, were crammed with bodies. Pushers, men who did exactly what the name implied, forced people onto the cars. At transfer points, lines of waiting people stretched for blocks. The few cars and buses were powered by charcoal burners attached at the rear. Bicycles, carts, and baby carriages transported goods too large or heavy to be carried in briefcases, knapsacks, or the omnipresent *furoshiki* or cloth wrapper—a cloth tied around an object to create a cover and carrying handle. To supplement rationed and black-market food, people planted garden patches in every conceivable spot.

Even though my trips in Nagoya and on excursions around the country furnished glimpses of the people and their lives, real conversations were limited because I could not speak Japanese and few Japanese could speak English. I was eager to learn, however, so I began attending weekly classes taught by Mr. Kenji Sasaki and sponsored by the Air Force. (In the journal I kept in Japan and in this book, I use courtesy titles with Japanese names to indicate gender and in deference to Japanese customs of politeness.) Although the course was discontinued six months later, it was useful to me to hear the language spoken correctly, and I learned some principles of pronunciation and usage. The existence of different words for women also became apparent in class, since our instruction manual was written for soldiers. Mr. Sasaki was apologetic every time we came upon words that should be used only by men, such as *benjo* for "toilet," whereas there was no mention of the term *gofujo*, literally "unclean place," the word for toilet used by women. Gradually, some words became a part of my Japanese vocabulary, especially because we often needed to know common words on trips. Once we had a hilarious experience when we wanted hot water for instant coffee. We knew that *atsui* meant "hot" and *mizu*, "water." But when we asked for *atsui mizu,* we received only perplexed looks from the maids until someone knowledgeable asked for *oyu*. We then learned that *mizu* meant "cold water." No wonder the maids were puzzled when we requested "hot cold water."

We had other communication problems. On a weekend trip to a rest hotel, we were served chocolate sundaes, a rare treat. After enjoying dessert and discovering that the table had no ashtray, I motioned to the waitress, held up a lighted cigarette, and said, "Ashtray, please." I was puzzled when she consulted the headwaiter about such a simple request, but I understood when she returned with another sundae. She had mistaken "ashtray" for "ice cream." Since I did not want to embarrass her or overlook such a windfall, I thanked her and ate the "ashtray."

About two months after my arrival in Nagoya, I was invited to speak to the English class at the all-male Nagoya College of Economics. I was told that I would speak to 250 men, most from families with business connections and some from farms, but all interested in American-English conversation.

Their instructor, Professor Suzuki—who had studied at Harvard University—gave me a copy of the text used in the college English classes: *The Little Yankee,* described as "a handbook of idiomatic American English treating of the daily life, customs and institutions of the United States with the vocabulary and phraseology incorporated in the text." I assured him that I would read it before visiting the college. When he spoke about giving me a gift in appreciation for my visit, I told him that, as a member of the occupation, I was not allowed to accept presents but that I looked forward with pleasure to meeting the students.

As I leafed through the 190-page book that evening, I was astounded. Unaware that English-language books had been forbidden in Japan for some years, I looked for a date in the book and discovered that the preface was written in 1921 and the book published in 1946. Even I, who was eleven in 1921, was surprised that the first chapter was devoted to "Calls" and contained such information as "Sunday is not the proper day for making formal calls." The second chapter, "Shops and Stores," told about harness, blacksmith, and tin shops. The book was impossible! I decided that in my talk I would update the information. If I began by talking about an American family, a safe subject, I could respond knowledgeably to questions.

On the designated day, Helen Cutting from the public relations office—in search of a story, I supposed—set off with me by jeep for the college. Professor Suzuki met us at the door and escorted us to the president's office to drink tea before my talk, the custom on such an occasion. The auditorium where I would speak seemed completely filled with young men dressed in school uniforms of blue or khaki, and I learned that one-third of the student body had come on their free time to hear English spoken by an American. As we entered at the rear, all rose. They remained standing until we reached the front of the auditorium. Then they sat down, and the professor introduced me in Japanese. I wondered what he said. When I took my place at the center of the platform behind a lectern, all the students rose again. There they stood facing me. "How do I get them down?" was my frantic thought. Maybe I should bow. I bowed awkwardly, as a foreigner would. They bowed gracefully, as they would, and then sat down.

Never had I faced a more attentive audience. They seemed to be trying to absorb every word. The professor, however, must have known their limitations, because after a few minutes he suggested that he would interpret in Japanese what I had said in English. The twenty minutes of my talk passed quickly, and then we were ready for questions. Professor Suzuki often had to help me understand what they were asking. And none of the questions had anything to do with family life in the United States, the subject of my remarks. Two questions I remember were "Do you think there will be coeducation in Japan?" and "Are there private colleges in the United States?"

Each student sat down after rising to ask his question. When I had answered, he rose again and said, "I understand what you said. Thank you." Perhaps this standard expression was meant to compliment me on the clarity of my expression. I rather doubted that he truly understood what I had said, but I nevertheless replied, "You are welcome." At the end of thirty minutes, I thanked them for coming and left the platform. All rose and remained standing as our procession of professor, speaker, and reporter marched to the back of the room and exited.

At the five more visits I made to the college—each time in an auditorium filled with earnest young men—the family, the home, and education were discussed. Two questions seemed to arouse particular interest: "In the United States, why is it necessary for women to study in the same college as men?" and "Do children settle a long way from home?"

Professor Suzuki and I had time for casual conversation after meetings while we waited for the jeep to pick me up. He once told me a joke about an American woman who was trying to learn to speak Japanese. The American woman, he said, was riding on a streetcar that lurched and threw her onto the lap of a seated male passenger. She was embarrassed, of course, and wanted to apologize. Although she meant to say *Gomen nasai* (Excuse me), the words she spoke were *Omedeto gozaimasu* (Congratulations). This was the only time I can recall during my years in Japan that a Japanese man told a joke.

My trips to the college were halted when our work schedule changed. But a short time later, Professor Suzuki invited me to visit the Noritake china factory, where I met a number of graduates of the college who held responsible positions. After we toured the factory, I was not surprised when I was presented with a tea set as thanks for my visits to the college. Under these circumstances, I felt it was all right for me to accept the gift.

During the time I was lecturing to these young men at the college, I was invited to give a talk at the Cultural Academy, a private college for young women. Mrs. Yukiko Sofue, whose beauty shop I often visited, arranged for the talk and accompanied me to the school. At the college, we were greeted by the principal, Mrs. Kato, dressed like Mrs. Sofue in kimono. We three sat around a table at one end of what I assumed was her office and had tea and cakes made by one of the students.

Then we joined the twenty-nine young women, aged about twenty, who sat around tables pushed together. Mrs. Sofue had told me that most of them were daughters of businessmen. All rose as we entered. Although Mrs. Sofue interpreted, I felt sure from their reactions that they understood some of what I said without interpretation. They were attentive and very shy, and they had no questions after I finished speaking. Some conversation did follow after I asked them what English books they had read and they answered *Daddy Longlegs, Little Women,* and *The Good Earth.* They said that books were very hard to get.

We three elders, followed by some students, then returned to Mrs. Kato's office for tea while waiting for the jeep. I learned that the students studied psychology, literature, cooking, sewing, homemaking, flower arrangement, the tea ceremony, and English. Each time a student walked down the corridor past the open door to the office, she bowed.

I was struck by the contrast between the two groups of students I met: the young women were reticent and shy, whereas the young men were self-assured and confident. Early in my stay in Japan, this contrast was an initial clue to the radical differences between the two genders there.

Teaching continued to offer me opportunities to meet Japanese citizens when I was invited to lead classes for two groups of men looking forward to the time when business relations with the United States would again be possible and a knowledge of English essential. In both cases, I was required to get permission from two sources: the military government, because I was teaching, and the military police, because meetings were held in off-limits buildings.

The first group consisted of officials in an industrial firm. We planned to meet after my workday ended, for an hour twice a week for nine months, and the firm rented a room in an inn for our meetings. After the first session, they wanted to pay me for my help, but I finally made them understand that Americans were forbidden to accept money or gifts from the Japanese and were not allowed to eat their scarce food. Such troublesome contradictions to Japanese custom were finally resolved when I agreed to accept a small gift as a token of appreciation and to join them for a meal on a special occasion.

Before the first class, I had been told that all of the men could read English and were able to speak it with varying degrees of fluency. The first meeting revealed that the degree for all was about zero. Having no experience in how to proceed, I began with simple words and phrases—"good morning, hello, good-bye"—read from typed sheets that I prepared for each class. The men progressed from practicing such elementary English words to reading paragraphs from magazines and books, still in varying degrees of fluency.

Aware that the reason for our meetings was to acquaint them with the United States, I led discussions on such subjects as hotels, trains, customs, meals, and homes. Because a practice in one country might be thought discourteous in the other, we talked about contrasting manners. In Japan, for example, slurping food showed appreciation; in the United States, it was considered bad manners. When struggling to put on my coat the first time, I mentioned that in my country, men assisted women with their coats. One replied, "This is a man's country." At the next meeting, however, when I reached for my coat, the same man removed it from the rack and held it for me. They must have made up a duty roster: during my time with them, each took a turn at this strange American custom.

After our first meetings, which were rather formal, the atmosphere became more relaxed and friendly. Perhaps they were embarrassed at times to be corrected, even kindly, by a woman—and an American. On the other hand, criticism may have been more acceptable to them because I was an American woman. The company president, an irregular attendee, contributed less than the others to conversations. I learned later that it was customary for a chief not to speak much before his subordinates, lest he say something to lose face.

Mr. Kyo Funaki, whom I got to know rather well and liked very much, was my star pupil and an exceptionally thoughtful individual. During cold months when we met in the unheated inn, I exchanged my street shoes for slipper-socks, whose soft soles did not harm the *tatami* (floor mats) but whose warmth helped keep my feet toasty. A week or so after the slipper-socks appeared, Mr. Funaki brought a cushion to class and put it on the cold floor for my feet as I changed from one kind of footwear to another.

After we had been acquainted some six months, he asked if I could obtain a book in English for him. I sent the request along to my mother, always my steadfast helper. About a month later he gave me two slim paperbacks on ceramics—*Human Elements in Ceramic Art* and *Iro-Nabeshima and Imayemon*—both of which I read with interest. When his book arrived, I gave it to him at a class meeting, considering the book a gift to repay him in part for his help to me. Two days later, I received a note from him, saying:

> In Japan, it is impolite to pay money to a superior so I would like to present something memorial to you. . . . You swept away my prejudices of Americans, you have the repose of a Buddhist image, you have oriental atmosphere. . . . Before I met you, I thought foreigners were flappers, especially seeing them walk on the Fifth Avenue of Nagoya. . . . I am very fond of you. I feel as if you were my aunt. I wish I were an American; if so, we would discuss many problems as equals.

I was touched by his words. I was also troubled. I did not think of myself as his "superior" (although he may have considered me to be so as his teacher); and he could certainly discuss "problems as equals" with this American. His mention of "something memorial" puzzled me then, although I soon forgot it. But a few weeks later, when I was invited to the home of some friends and met Mr. Funaki's father, the words came back to me. The senior Funaki presented me with an Imari plate from his son. It was certainly "something memorial": a plate with a design of maple leaves in fall coloring made and signed by Imayemon, the ceramist who was the subject of one of the books he gave me.

The second group of Japanese men I taught were bankers. I noted in my journal that the two men who visited me to arrange for a twice-weekly class in conversational English "assured me that the men were a high-class group, gentlemen, and that I need not be worried about meeting with them." As if I would be! Nothing was said about payment for my help, which led me to think that some conversation must have taken place with the industrialists about how this troublesome matter had been settled before.

All bank business stopped when I arrived for the first session. Curious glances were directed our way as my escort and I walked through the silent ground-floor room to the meeting place upstairs. Waiting there were ten young men and the manager: "all very eager and a most intelligent-looking group, all well dressed," I recorded in my journal. I used the same method of teaching with the bankers as I'd used with the industrialists.

One day when only four members were present, we talked about money. I had four pennies with me, which I distributed and they examined intently. After one asked if he could keep the penny, I said they all could if they wanted to. Then when I commented that I would probably be sent to prison for giving them American money, they looked very distressed until they realized I was joking. After a question arose about what a cookie was, I took a box of cookies from the PX to the next class. They each took one and put them on their papers, eating only when I urged them to do so to find out what a cookie tasted like.

When I knew early in July that I would be leaving Nagoya the following month, I told the class myself rather than letting them hear of it secondhand. At the next-to-last meeting, I was presented with a tea set to thank me for my help. It was a duplicate of the one I'd received from the college.

As a result of these and other experiences during that first year in Nagoya, supplemented by my next three and a half years on

Shikoku, I began to understand the monumental challenges facing the occupation. Our mission was to help the people learn how to exercise democratic practices, including equal rights for men and women. Although Japan had a democracy in the sense of an elected parliamentary form of government before the war, what was missing, in both societal and political senses, was equality. Of the many long-standing authoritarian traditions that presented obstacles to achieving democracy, none was more important than the subordination of the individual to the group. This concept is illustrated, very simply, by the contrast between Japanese and American forms of address on an envelope:

Japanese	*American*
U.S.A.	Miss Mary Smith
Illinois	1234 S. Elm St.
Chicago	Chicago
1234 S. Elm St.	Illinois
Smith Mary	U.S.A.

For the Japanese, the individual's name is the last thing to identify her, while in the United States it is the first.

Another tradition was the pervasiveness of hierarchy. The Japanese constantly demonstrated in subtle gestures and language their awareness of differences between people who seemed to me to be equals. In my English class, for example, one of the businessmen was a lawyer, but he said that he felt inferior to another class member who was a *sensei,* or teacher. And one day from my office window, as I watched two elderly ladies dressed in kimono meet on the street, an almost imperceptible delay before the second woman bowed showed that she held the higher position of the two.

A third traditional concept was filial piety—respect for one's ancestors. Married women also were subjected to the redirection of their filial piety to their in-laws' families. Women were exhorted in a standard handbook, "It is the chief duty of a girl living in the parental house to practice filial piety toward her father and mother. But after marriage, her chief duty is to honor her father-in-law and mother-in-law, to honor them beyond her own father and mother, to love and reverence them with all ardor, and to tend them with practice of every filial piety." Women frequently asked me why the young wife who lived with her husband's parents and suffered under the strict rule of her mother-in-law could then, when she became the mother-in-law, treat her young daughter-in-law the same way she had deplored as a young wife. I had no idea how to answer.

Finally, traditional modes of making decisions and conducting meetings were also contrary to democratic practices. Because of the many restrictive aspects of Japanese culture, individuals arrived at independent decisions only with great difficulty. Even more daunting for many was taking responsibility for making a decision that required action as a consequence. One example involved what was proper for me to present Mrs. Honda, a prominent leader, as a memorial upon the death of her husband. As I wrote in my journal:

> Yesterday it was decided that ¥200 (approximately fifty-five cents) from me and ¥100 from the others [would be proper]. The men in the team office where one of the women worked then thought that ¥200 was not enough, but the women decided any more would seem too much. So today, when I called [my assistant at the team], she said they had decided I should take flowers instead of money. That was all right with me. But when she came over from the team, the decision again was money. She had heard that Mrs. Honda had been having a hard time, even doing work at home. I was agreeable. Then she said that ¥200 was not enough—¥500 from me would be better.

I found it interesting, to say the least, that not only was this decision so hard to reach but that the final increase was because of my position as an American with the occupation. Whether I could afford that or any amount was never a factor. The only question was its appropriateness.

Strong feelings of class distinctions, lack of individuality, and the desire for conformity—fostered over many years by the government, schools, and families—led members of organizations and public bodies to continue to embrace a system that seemed thoroughly undemocratic to me. In the 1990s, the standard interpretation of decisionmaking methods in Japan is that decisions are made only after long discussions in which all members' opinions are fully aired. But the Japanese I observed in those postwar years typically shrank from open debate that might be acrimonious or might discredit the leader. In an organization, votes were seldom—perhaps never—taken, and the role of chairmen was crucial, often decisive, as they summarized the feelings of the group when they felt agreement had been reached. A chairman noted for his ability as a leader was said to have *haragei*, literally "belly art" or "intuition." I always asked how a leader with *haragei* would know, for example, if members of an organization preferred that a booklet cover be blue, or perhaps green. No adequate answer was ever given, but I was often told that the question "did not fit the Japanese situation."

3 · · ·

Women

Called

"Oi"

L ong before the end of my year in Nagoya, I became sharply
aware that the status of men in Japan was higher than that of
women and learned that the subordinate position of women—
like many other social beliefs and practices—grew out of long-
standing traditions of marriage and family. An early example
occurs in a story of the original marriage ceremony in the *Kojiki*
(Records of Ancient Matters). Completed in A.D. 712, this volume contains what some say are accounts of the divine age and
what others call myths. Long, long ago, the deities Izanagi, His
Augustness the Male-Who-Invites, and Izanami, Her Augustness
the Female-Who-Invites,

> standing upon the Floating Bridge of Heaven, pushed
> down the jeweled spear and stirred the brine until it went
> curdle-curdle, and drew the spear up. The brine that
> dripped down from the end of the spear was piled up and
> became an island. . . . Having descended from heaven onto
> this island, they saw to the erection of a heavenly august
> pillar. . . . Now the male deity turning by the left, and the
> female deity by the right, they went around the pillar sep-

arately. When they met together on the one side, the female deity spoke first, "What a charming and lovely youth." The male deity then spoke, "What a charming and lovely maiden." After they had finished their first speaking, the male deity said, "I am male and by right should have spoken first. This was unlucky. Let us two go around again." Upon this the two deities went back, and having met anew, this time the male deity spoke first. . . . Hereupon the male and female first became united as husband and wife.

This story clearly shows sexism in Japan's creation myths, although actual marriage patterns in the classical era (until about A.D. 1200) related to the residence of a wife's, rather than husband's, kin group, and inheritance was generally on the female side. Sexist marriage customs that limited women's opportunities and lowered their status were, however, intensified in the late medieval period.

The almost complete absence of women's names in the written histories of Japan illustrates another form of inequality. Historians would no doubt mention a few empresses as important figures; I would list two writers. Sometime between 1008 and 1020, Shikibu Murasaki, a court lady, wrote a long novel, *Genji Monogatari* (The Tale of Genji), one of the world's classics. In it, she has a young prince speak of woman as "in every way inferior to man . . . regarded as the principal cause of human sin." Shonagon Sei, born ca. 966, was best known for her *Makura no Soshi* (Pillow Book)—the name given diaries in which random thoughts were written. In it, she recorded facts that gave a picture of the time in which she lived.

After the feudal period, the status of women—especially in the elite classes—reached a very low level in the Tokugawa period (1615–1868), largely because of the rise of Confucianism and the power of its emphasis on ancestor worship, filial piety, and the superiority of men over women. *Onna Daigaku* (Greater Learning for Women), a small volume written in simple language attributed to Confucian scholar Ekken Kaibara (1630–1714), strengthened the concept of the inferiority of women. Some excerpts exemplify its main points:

> The only qualities that befit a woman are gentle obedience, chastity, mercy, and quietness. . . . A wife has no particular lord. She must look to her husband as her lord, and must serve him with all worship and reverence, not despising or thinking lightly of him. The great lifelong duty of a woman is obedience. . . . When the husband issues his instructions, the wife must never disobey them. . . . Without her husband's permission, she must go nowhere, neither should she make any gift on her own responsibility. . . . The five worst infirmities that afflict the female are indocility, discontent, slander, jealousy, and silliness. Without any doubt, these five infirmities are found in seven or eight out of every ten women, and it is from these that arises the inferiority of women to men.

Partly because few books were available for women, this little volume was widely read when it was first written and for more than two hundred years was considered a suitable gift for a bride. A woman elected to the Diet (the Japanese legislature) after the war even recalled that her grandfather had left her a beautiful edition of the book in his will—although she admitted that she found it a strange present for a girl. She, however, lived in Tokyo, and I suspect that women in more conservative areas of Japan would not have thought it so strange.

In the family, the tradition was that the husband and father ruled, and then passed this prerogative on to the eldest son, who remained in the house to raise his children and take care of his aged parents. As the one responsible for the behavior of family members, the father was the final authority on all questions. His status put him at the honored position at the table when meals were served and at the head of the line for the family bath. The wife obeyed her husband, was responsible for running the household, and held a low position in the family hierarchy. The differences between the names used in the family indicated the gap between the positions of husband and wife: he called her by her first name; she never called him by his first name, but used a respectful term such as *anata* (you). If they had children, *okasan* (mother) and *otosan* (father) were commonly heard.

Distasteful to me because it lacked respect and dignity was the brusque "*oi!*" (you!) the husband sometimes used to address his wife. When I spoke to women's groups later on Shikoku, applause almost invariably followed a statement such as "democracy cannot exist in the home when you are still addressed by your husband as '*oi.*'"

As a foreigner, I found strange the custom by which parents with no sons would adopt their eldest daughter's husband to carry on the family name. Problems and strained relations often resulted from such adoptions, as the positions of the young husband and wife were difficult. One woman married to an adopted husband told me she had wanted to go to college; but since she was the eldest daughter, her marriage was important and, therefore, she was not supposed to know more than the man she would marry. This may have been an unusual case, for daughters who stayed in the family were more likely to be better educated than daughters who married out, since a daughter who married out drained family resources when she took her education with her to a new family.

Conditions for women were supposed to change under Japan's new constitution, which went into effect in May 1947 and guaranteed equal rights for men and women:

> All of the people are equal under the law and there shall be
> no discrimination in political, economic or social relations,

because of race, creed, sex, social status or family origin (Article 14).

Other articles gave women the right to vote, guaranteed legal equality and equal education for both sexes, and provided that

> Marriage shall be based only on the mutual consent of both sexes and it shall be maintained through mutual coopera-tion with the equal rights of husband and wife as the basis. With regard to choice of spouse, property rights, inheri-tance, choice of domicile, divorce and other matters per-taining to marriage and family, laws shall be enacted from the standpoint of individual dignity and the essential equal-ity of the sexes (Article 24).

The constitution gave women equality on paper, but could the customs and traditions so deeply rooted in the past be changed to comply with legal requirements? This issue became of central importance to me as I prepared to take what I had learned in Nagoya and go on to my next job as a women's affairs officer with the civil education branch of the military government. Where could my colleagues and I begin to explain to Japanese women the legal rights to which they were now entitled? Our initial instruction from our supervisors—and a wise move, I thought —was to go to women where they already were meeting together. That usually meant the *fujinkai*, women's clubs already in existence in villages, cities, and prefectures. There we would begin the informal education that these women now needed to assume their places of equality.

Women's organizations in late 1940s Japan bore little resem-blance to those I knew in the United States, where social clubs and interest groups were often not affiliated with any other group and were generally independent of governmental control or direction. In Japan, the government had established the Social Education Bureau (Shakai Kyoikukyoku) in 1929 as part of the

Ministry of Education. Its responsibilities included encouraging and even forming social education organizations, including ones for boys and girls, young people, and women.

Even before that time, the Patriotic Women's Association (Aikoku Fujinkai) had been formed in 1901. In 1931, the Greater Japan Federation of Women's Organizations (Dai Nippon Rengo Fujinkai) was founded and, in 1932, the National Defense Women's Association (Kokubo Fujinkai). In 1942, the three were combined by cabinet directive into one association, called the Greater Japan Women's Association (Dai Nippon Fujinkai), under direction of the military. Aside from government-sponsored *fujinkai*, independent women's organizations—many with re-formist and progressive agendas—had earlier existed in Japan, but were forced out of existence by the militarist government in the late 1930s and early 1940s.

During World War II, women were placed in war jobs of all kinds: they dug trenches for bomb shelters, took part in air-raid drills, and worked in patriotic associations. The kimono was discarded for *mompe*—loose, baggy trousers that proved much more practical for wartime. The national government subsidized the national association and required every woman to be a dues-paying member. This thoroughly undemocratic system continued officially until the end of the war: the national organization directed activities down through various levels of federations—prefectural, *gun* (a government unit comparable to the U.S. county), and city or town—all the way to the local groups. Still, although all women were listed as members, few attended the infrequent meetings. In other words, these women's organizations were neither social nor educational but simply tools the militarists used to carry on the war effort.

After the war, the new Japanese leaders made many changes, purging (i.e., removing from office) many social education officials and others who were no longer considered acceptable. The national women's association, as a militaristic organization, was dissolved. However, two official directives issued in November 1945, "Women's Cultural Establishment" (Hatsu Sha No. 27) and "Women's Cultural Institutes" (Hatsu Sha No. 15), showed little change from prewar edicts—except that democracy, instead of loyalty to the emperor, was now the objective of social education. Thus, most *fujinkai* in the immediate postwar period were simply the same old compulsory groups—with the same wartime leaders, and with all women feeling compelled to be members as they had been before.

The new Social Education Law (No. 207, 1949), passed by the Diet on May 22, 1949, was designed to change this situation. It clearly set forth the place of government relative to all social education agencies. Two important provisions were

> The state and local public bodies shall by no means take controlling leadership over organizations relating to social education nor interfere with them in their activities (Article 12).
>
> The state and local public bodies shall give no subsidies to organizations relating to social education (Article 13).

The passage of this major legislation officially opened the way for postwar social education organizations to operate without government control and without subsidies that might obligate the receivers to follow the directions of those who gave them.

Even in 1947, when I had a survey done of the *fujinkai*, the results demonstrated that little change had occurred in women's groups since the end of the war. I learned that:

- Some of the present women leaders had also been wartime leaders.
- Men were still presidents of most women's organizations.
- The membership was predominantly housewives.
- Organizations had large paper memberships, but few actually attended meetings.

- Meetings were held infrequently.
- Parliamentary procedures, such as the requirement that decisions should be made by vote of members, were not understood.

I couldn't help wondering if the occupation would last long enough to turn the *fujinkai* into organizations that would respond to their members' interests and needs.

My intense education in the role and status of Japanese women came only partly from books, documents, and official meetings. Much more important was my acquaintance, starting that first year, with individual women. In Nagoya, I came to know best these three: Sadako, a maid in our hotel; Kyoko Nakano, an interpreter; and Yukiko Sofue, a businesswoman.

I met Sadako through Helen Cutting, my reporter friend from the public relations office. When Helen had arrived at the Chiyoda Hotel in the fall, she had been distressed to learn she must share a room. During the war, she had been crowded together with many others in Santo Tomas prison in the Philippines during its occupation by the Japanese, and a private room now seemed a necessity to her. After the hotel manager promised she could have a room by herself if she found vacant space, Helen located an empty closet; it had been used to store brooms but was large enough to serve as a small single room with a metal cot, a table, a folding chair, and a rod behind a curtain to hold clothes. When Helen was transferred to Tokyo, she offered me the broom closet, with the proviso that I help the hotel maid with English. This maid had been attending an English class, and Helen was giving her additional help. The prospect of having a room by myself was irresistible, and I eagerly agreed.

After moving into the broom closet, I began regular sessions with the maid, whom Helen called Dimples. Her name was Sadako, and I felt she should be addressed by that. She was twenty-three, had a good mind, and was eager to learn, often staying long after her work was finished to practice English. She was ambitious and, after about six weeks, she talked to me about her desire to take typing lessons. Since she had no time for classes, she planned to resign the hotel job and work for two women as their personal maid. She asked if she could also work for me without pay if I would continue to help her with English. Although I felt no need for the services of a personal maid, I proposed to pay her the same salary as each of the others and continue with lessons as before.

After a month's trial, she confessed that her plans were not working out because the other two Americans gave her so much to do that she had little time for her studies. We had a long conversation, during which she told me about her family. Her father, aged fifty-six, did not work; a sister, twenty-two, also did not work; one brother was in school. In spite of these problems, Sadako soon quit working for the other two women to devote more time to her classes. Later, however, she changed her mind and decided to work as a maid in the home of an American family. After only a short time, she changed her mind again, telling me she would continue working for me and not for the family.

For about three weeks, we continued our schedule, until a long talk explained her indecision of the past month: "Sadako is very unhappy these days," I noted in my journal, "because her sister is ill with heart trouble and will never be all right. Sadako has to take care of her besides earning her living. I don't know what, if anything, I can do for her. She must work but has had to give up her typing and English lessons. Her family wants her to marry an older man with money. I didn't even try to give an opinion." With that conversation, our relationship ended, as she never returned. Of course, I worried about her and her troubles. After she tried so hard to learn English and typing to improve her status as a working woman, did she marry the older man because that course seemed the only one left for her? One evening before her departure, I returned to my room after dinner and found a box from Sadako containing a large pottery figure of a sacred lion, a charm against evil. The lion now stands on my bookshelf as a reminder of her.

The first professional woman I met in Nagoya was Kyoko Nakano, interpreter at the Chiyoda Hotel. This widow, whose husband had died fighting in the Philippines, was quiet and unassuming but always helpful and pleasant. Mrs. Nakano and I met often in the hotel dining room and lobby and in my room. When she came to the dining room while I was eating, I always invited her to join me. One evening, after we'd eaten together, we moved to the lobby to talk and she told me of her ambition to organize women to improve their lot. About a month later, she asked me to remain at the table after dinner. According to my journal, "She told me an American man had approached her to be his 'girl friend,' as she put it. He said his wife and three children were not here, nor was her husband. He told her such arrangements are quite common in the United States. I tried to explain, but couldn't explain away his poor taste in his approach to her." I was not naive, of course, and I knew that American men made such arrangements with Japanese women. And I certainly realized that an American could offer essentials such as food and clothing, as well as luxuries like cosmetics and jewelry that were unattainable to most Japanese at the time. However, I could not and would not advise her. I told her only that, in my part of society in my country, such arrangements were not countenanced.

Near the end of my year in Nagoya, Mrs. Nakano and I had two long talks in my room. She started the first after reading an article in an American magazine that said many more women in the United States were now drinking. She "wondered about that because we were victors in the war." I reminded her that "even victors paid for a war—men were killed in battle, families were broken, houses were scarce. I believe she feels the United States has everything; it is hard for her to realize what the true situation is." Then she asked if England was "bad off, too," and I replied that food was scarce there, as in Japan, and items were rationed. When she asked whether black markets existed in England, I told her I did not know. "The Japanese should be ashamed since their black market is so bad," she responded.

At our second long talk, she asked if I thought the earth would ever be one world without countries. She seemed satisfied with my saying that I did not believe the world was ready for that yet. I must have felt that we knew each other well enough by that time for me to ask her a question: what had the Japanese leaders promised the people if Japan won the war? Her reply was not unexpected: "Japan will be the chief country in Asia and will have enough room then for people to emigrate." She had no answer to my point that "people won't even emigrate in their own country to Hokkaido," an area not heavily populated. That led her to say that another answer given by leaders was that there would be less poverty after Japan won the war. She said, "Our leaders thought that the United States had so much they would not fight."

"Japan should have known better than that," I said, "after it attacked our fleet, killing our men, at the same time it was talking peace at the White House. Americans could not forget that."

"Americans had everything."

"No, we had poor people, too."

"But no beggars," she announced firmly.

"Of course we did," I replied.

"I read that one thing that was impressive about the United States was that there were no beggars."

"Who wrote that?" I asked. "A Japanese?"

"Yes."

"I can show you beggars in America."

She continued, "Before the war, most of the people you met on the street had enough to eat and wear and a place to live. But now people are hungry—even starving."

"The Americans here," I said, "know that the Japanese now are more interested in being housed, clothed, and fed than in what Mr. Katayama is doing as prime minister."

"Yes, that is true. My father says that, at the barber shop, the men used to talk politics, but now only about where to get food."

More than once during the year, Mrs. Nakano invited me to her parents' home, which they shared with her and her small son, plus a daughter-in-law and her two sons who were awaiting a move to Tokyo. Their tiny home was on the grounds of a Shinto shrine, where they had moved after losing their house and belongings in bombings. I already knew her father, Mr. Sasaki, for he had been my Japanese instructor at the Air Force training school. Mrs. Sasaki, Mrs. Nakano's mother, was the only Japanese "lady" I met in Nagoya—meaning an older woman devoted to the duties of a housewife and apparently satisfied with her modest, self-effacing role. On this social call, she acted as hostess, first serving ordinary tea and then preparing ceremonial tea after the subject came up in our conversation.

When the family invited me to dinner a month later, Mr. Sasaki prepared the meal of sukiyaki at the table. Then his wife waited on us while we ate; when not serving us, she remained in the kitchen. The discussion among Mr. Sasaki, his daughter, and me turned to *No,* Japan's classical drama. Mr. Sasaki, remarking that his wife knew some of the singing parts, called her in from the kitchen. While our conversation continued in English, she sat nearby and sang for a long time until her husband dismissed her.

When I first met Yukiko Sofue at her beauty shop, little did I realize the variety of experiences that our acquaintance would open. As she had attended a college of English in Tokyo, she spoke and understood the language well. Before the war, she had operated a shop at the Kanko Hotel, where she served American women who were university teachers or wives of businessmen. When Americans returned to Nagoya during the occupation, she opened a beauty shop in the Chiyoda Hotel.

She had arranged for me to speak to the young women attending the Cultural Academy, and later she invited me to attend a reunion of women from her college, about a dozen of whom lived in Nagoya. When I agreed, she asked me to invite some other American women to join us. The reunion was held in a former bank building partially destroyed by bombing. Wearing our coats, we sat on the floor around a long table covered with blankets. When we put our feet under the table and the blankets over our laps, our feet were kept warm by heat from under the table. I was curious about the source of the heat and peeked under the covers—inconspicuously, I hoped—to discover an electric toaster. We were served tea and three kinds of cakes, two made from sweet potatoes and one from red beans, both common ingredients in Japanese cakes. Because the Japanese women seemed shy and we Americans were at a loss to know what to talk about, there were long pauses of silence. When they asked us to sing a Christmas song, we chose "Silent Night." Some of the Japanese women joined in. Then in response to our request, they sang the song of their alma mater. Next on our program was "White Christmas," followed by a folk song from them. In spite of some awkwardness, our visit passed quickly and pleasurably. I gave the hostesses a tin of candy.

On another occasion, Mrs. Sofue invited six of us to join six of them for a tea ceremony. After a short walk, we turned in at a very ordinary-looking doorway to find a lovely garden and the home of a male teacher of the tea ceremony. We soon were seated along one side of the room, with time first to admire the flower arrangement in the *tokonoma* (alcove) of one camellia bud and two branches and the *kakemono* (hanging scroll) of a winter scene. Then one young woman prepared the ceremonial tea and two others—no doubt students—served; the master and his wife sat next to the one performing the ceremony. The Americans were served first, one at a time, and then the Japanese, in a ceremony that took all afternoon.

My last meeting with this group of women took place on a bright, cold, and windy day in March, when we walked several miles to a small Buddhist temple served by a priestess instead of the usual priest. Adjoining the immaculate temple was the house of the nun, where the others were already gathered. We were served ceremonial tea—very strong and very hot—in the tea room. This Buddhist priestess, who neither spoke nor understood English, was beautifully robed, with a shaven head. I was very impressed with her because she occupied a place of honor and was a leader in her own right.

One evening in my room, Mrs. Sofue told me about attending a meeting of women's organizations. I noted in my journal that she "was disappointed because so little was accomplished. The women spent so much time arguing about unimportant things and not even talking about the big things. For example, they argued for more than thirty minutes about whether the secretary should be called secretary or clerk. 'The women are so conservative and narrow-minded,' she said, 'most of them teachers— never a very radical group.'" I tried to encourage her by suggesting that her point of view might be broader than others' because of her long acquaintance with foreigners. At this point, I knew very little about Japanese women's organizations, but I learned later that the common practice of arguing about unimportant things and ignoring the big things stemmed from old procedures in which Japanese customarily followed directions from someone in authority and did not carry on association business themselves.

After an event near the end of my year in Nagoya, I wrote in my journal, "There was Mrs. Sofue with painted toenails." This succinct comment was not meant to be frivolous. Rather it was a reminder that at least one Japanese woman was independent enough to be that different in such a traditional society.

As I took all I had learned from the women of Nagoya and prepared for my assignment as a women's affairs officer on Shikoku,

I was thus aware of some of the obstacles ahead in helping the Japanese achieve a government of all the people. I was not sure how the future would emerge from the past, with its long history of custom and tradition; but I was secure in my belief in the good will of the women, and I was optimistic that we could work together under the constitution toward a democratic Japan. Was I naive to face the future with such confidence? In retrospect, I must confess that I was not fully aware of the monumental conflict between past and future that the occupation represented to the women of Japan.

4 · · ·

First

Meetings

on Shikoku

B y June 1947, I knew that I wanted to remain in Japan after
my appointment in Nagoya ended, but I hoped to find a more
challenging job than that of a clerk-typist. In July, I visited Eighth
Army Headquarters in Yokohama, under whose jurisdiction the
military government fell, knowing by then that Civil Information
and Education (CI&E) would be the section that might have a
place for me. When I outlined my qualifications and then said
that I would prefer not to be located in a large city after spending a year in Nagoya, my two interviewers exchanged quick
glances. They pointed out the negative aspects of being assigned
to an isolated area: I might be the only American woman working in the military government, and I might be far from sources
of supply such as a good PX. When I said that neither of those
bothered me, they told me that I had been accepted for the
Shikoku Military Government Region on Shikoku, the smallest
of Japan's four main islands. "One of the best men," they said, had
already been sent as head of the civil education section, and I
would be the women's affairs officer and the only female staff
member on the island. Two benefits of the location were mentioned: a beach for swimming in the Inland Sea and a boat for

sailing. Neither of those appealed to me, but I was excited to learn that I would be working with many groups of Japanese, especially in women's organizations.

Orders in hand, I left Nagoya on August 19, 1947, for several days of training in Yokohama. Even though I did almost the same work the entire time I was on Shikoku, my job title changed from training instructor to education specialist, then to educationalist (social education) and to educationalist (general)—all professional-level positions with no civil service status. The beginning grade was 7, at a yearly salary of $4,246; the final was 11, at $5,400. The differential of 25 percent for a hardship post in 1946 was reduced to 10 percent January 1, 1949, and discontinued by March 3, 1950. By that time, working conditions in Japan were considered to be no different from those in the United States—a judgment most likely made by someone living in the Tokyo-Yokohama area who had never visited Shikoku.

My training consisted mostly of reading documents related to the occupation and being briefed at the CI&E office. I also had my first contact with a women's affairs officer already at work with a military government team. Even after talking with her, however, how I would begin my work was not clear. Could it be that no one really knew exactly what we were to do to implement the transition from military to civilian government?

When my train departed from Yokohama on August 25 about half-past eight in the evening, for the first time since leaving Chicago I had a lower berth. When ready for sleep, I put up my window shade to get some air and noticed a fine screen covering the window. In spite of that guard against cinders, in the morning the end of my pillow by the window was covered with black residue from the coal-burning locomotive. During the night, after my eyes became accustomed to the dark, I saw many little lights in the fields. Although they looked like big fireflies, I learned later that they were simple shallow bowls supported on tripods and filled with a combustible liquid that attracted insects harmful to rice plants. Unfortunately, I was told, these make-shift traps made necessary by the lack of insecticides were quite ineffective.

Early in the morning, we passed Nagoya, then went on to Kyoto and through Osaka and Kobe. When we reached Okayama, I disembarked. I was then in "foreign territory" in Chugoku Region, which like Shikoku was occupied by the British Commonwealth Occupation Force (BCOF). In theory, all of the victorious nations occupied Japan: Australia, Canada, China, France, Great Britain, India, the Netherlands, New Zealand, the Philippines, the Soviet Union, and the United States, joined by Burma and Pakistan after their independence. But in actuality, the occupation was almost entirely the responsibility of the United States. When I arrived on Shikoku, BCOF controlled two regions: Chugoku, in the western section of the largest island of Honshu (occupied by troops from Australia and New Zealand), and the small island of Shikoku (occupied by troops from England and India). After BCOF troops left, no American reinforcements were sent, leaving the regions without any occupying troops.

As a consequence of this occupation structure, the two American military government regions and their prefectural teams in Chugoku and Shikoku were directly under Eighth Army. Those in the rest of the country were under either the I or IX Corps, headquartered in Kyoto and Sendai, respectively. Simply stated, Chukogu and Shikoku regions had one layer of American command fewer than the rest of the country—an advantage for which occupation officials on Shikoku were grateful.

The next lap of the trip took about an hour by train from Okayama to Uno, the port on the shore of the Inland Sea. "The landscape is different in this part of the country," I noted in my journal. "There are more rocky promontories and sandy hillsides than I've seen [before]." On the hour-long ferry ride across the Inland Sea to our destination, Takamatsu, I sat with other passengers in the prow in space reserved for the occupation force, furnished with comfortable chairs and benefited by a cool breeze. The sea, deep blue, was dotted with islands, most of which were green with trees and other vegetation. One island was shaped like a huge chocolate drop.

The word *Shi-koku,* meaning "four countries," originated in the division of the island into four prefectures (comparable to U.S. states), now called Ehime, Kagawa, Kochi, and Tokushima. Bounded on the north by the Inland Sea and on the south by the Pacific Ocean, Shikoku has a climate that is mild because of the Japanese current. Kochi, the southernmost prefecture, is the only place in Japan where two crops of rice are grown each year. Farming, fishing, and salt manufacture from sea water were the island's chief occupations, with a bit of small-scale industry. Because most of the island is mountainous, the population was concentrated near the coastline.

In size and population, Shikoku was then comparable to the state of Massachusetts. The island's area is 8,248 acres; in 1950, its population was about 4.2 million. Prefectural figures were Ehime, 1,522,000; Kagawa, 945,000; Kochi, 838,000; and Tokushima, 878,000. In other ways—transportation, for one—Shikoku was definitely not comparable to Massachusetts. Although railroads and buses operated, people often walked miles to reach a rail or bus line. Some of the smaller islands that are politically part of Shikoku were accessible only by fishing boats. Rail travel was slow, since trains stopped at every town on the line and routes were circuitous because of the mountains. Roads were narrow and winding, so bus travel was equally slow.

As a result of the island's inaccessibility, contacts with outsiders had always been limited. Very few Japanese from the other islands visited, and Shikoku residents seldom even traveled around their own island. I later learned that when staff members from Takamatsu accompanied Americans on field trips, they were usually visiting the other prefectures for the first time. This isolation largely continued during the occupation. American troops that had landed at Komatsushima in November 1945 were withdrawn when BCOF troops moved into Chugoku and Shikoku, so the only Americans on the island when I arrived were with either the military government or small counterintelligence units. Ironically, this situation had its advantages for occupation personnel like me who wanted to interact more freely with the local people, because unlike in Nagoya or Tokyo, where large numbers of occupation troops were stationed and many areas were off-limits, on Shikoku there were no military police and no constraints on visits to such places as theaters, movie houses, and inns.

The military government on Shikoku was composed of a region (with overall management responsibility) with four teams under it—one for each prefecture. Offices for the region and for the Kagawa team were in Takamatsu, capital of Kagawa Prefecture. The other teams were located in the other prefectures' capital cities: Matsuyama in Ehime, Kochi city in Kochi, and Tokushima city in Tokushima. Each team was under a military commander, and officers and enlisted men were assigned to various sections as needed for operations. Members of both the regional and team staffs covered all phases of life: civil education, including women's affairs; civil information; economics, including labor; legal and government; public health; and public welfare. Early in the occupation, all section chiefs had been military men because posts were assigned to whoever was on the scene regardless of experience. As time passed, civilian experts in education and training were recruited to take over positions formerly held by the military. When I arrived on Shikoku, regional section heads were civilian men, with the exception of one captain; I became the first woman staff member. Since there were no other women's affairs officers, my responsibility covered both the region and the prefectures. As a member of the regional staff, I would be based in Takamatsu and travel from there to the other areas.

Housing arrangements for Americans varied from city to city, but in all cases, single officers and civilians were quartered in large houses or residential buildings. Accommodations for dependent families were either new houses built by the Japanese government or renovated, undamaged Japanese homes. Japanese people—their salaries paid by their government—were employed, often far below their capabilities, as drivers, cooks, waiters, maids, and office workers. Once a week, a commissary train visited the four capital cities to deliver groceries and staples ordered by families the previous week and to provide food and supplies to military units. One coach offered postal and banking services. For supplies between visits of the train, there was a small PX in each city.

Getting around the island was not easy for Americans. Local travel was almost entirely by jeep; staff cars were available for the commanding officers. Occupation personnel could travel by train in a half-coach that ran only once a day between Takamatsu and the other three capitals. The trip to Kochi city held the record: one hundred miles took six hours, and the train passed through 103 tunnels. To supplement this regular service, a railroad coach that could be attached to any train was provided for the region. The coach used in 1947, called The Eagle, contained eight double-decker metal cots, tables, chairs, toilet, shower, and kitchen space. If a group traveled on The Eagle, regular meals were prepared by cooks from the regional mess. When I used the special coach alone, rations from the mess hall were my main source of food; the car boy warmed meals on a charcoal brazier. Americans who needed to reach spots not on a railroad line journeyed by jeep. For travel to islands, small boats were allocated to the region and each team.

When I arrived in Takamatsu on August 26, 1947, Fred Kerlinger met me at the ferry dock. Fred was tall and thin and about my age; as chief of the regional civil education section, he was my new boss. Clutched in his hands were two sandwiches and a can of juice—my lunch for an unexpected final stage of my journey. He told me that I was to go on immediately by train to Tokushima Prefecture. I would stay there with the team until September 15, when a dependent house was to be ready in Takamatsu. Fred and I sorted out my luggage, some to accompany me but the balance to be put in storage. As the train pulled away from the station, I could only laugh to myself at this change of plans.

The fifty-mile trip took about two and a half hours. First we rode through mountains, then suddenly with a great rattling of windows passed on a single track through tunnels, to emerge again in farmland. I was met at the station by a sergeant with a jeep and learned we were still not at our destination. Team members lived about eight miles south of the capital near the town of Komatsushima, one of the chief ports of entry to the island. We arrived at the team compound just in time for dinner, which I ate with the officers in their mess hall in a large Japanese house that also contained the billet and mess hall for enlisted men. The bachelor officers' quarters (BOQ) and recently built houses for married men with dependents were clustered nearby. The land, formerly the home of a feudal lord, was the estate of a wealthy Japanese man, Mr. Tada; the compound was known as Tada House. By the time I unpacked a little, pressed a dress, had my bath, and wrote about my day, the hour was late. I recorded in my diary:

> As I sit here all alone in a dependent house complete with upstairs and downstairs, I can hear the water washing up from the ocean against the seawall—only a few yards away. I am living in a house of seven rooms, temporarily I

believe, a two-story unit, the adjoining unit occupied by a
sergeant, wife, and son. The whole place is right on the
seashore. Looking out toward the water from the house,
you look through pine trees. I must say this is a beautiful
spot.

The seven-room house was not mine long, as after five days I
was moved next door into the adjoining one-story unit of five
rooms. During my time there, furniture disappeared piece by
piece as my unit was cannibalized for family housing. After three
weeks, I was moved back to the guest room of the house where
I had first stayed.

The value of being part of the team and observing operations
on the lowest level of military government became apparent
even on the first day when I joined the group of some twenty
enlisted men, six American officers, an Australian warrant officer from BCOF, and one male civilian. Three wives and two
children also lived at Tada House when I arrived. The commanding officer was a lieutenant colonel; the chief of my section,
CI&E (Civil Information and Education), was a major; others
who headed sections were captains and the one civilian; and the
assistant economics officer, who handled labor and procurement,
was the warrant officer. The headquarters building was located
in the center of Tokushima city, which along with the other three
capital cities had been bombed in an air raid on July 4, 1945.
Leaflets dropped by U.S. planes had told people what day the
bombs would be dropped, so most had streamed out of the cities
before that day. But when the police forced them to return to
fight fires, great loss of life and many injuries resulted. Although
the four capitals and other Shikoku cities were badly damaged,
the devastation was not as overwhelming as in Tokyo, Yokohama,
and Nagoya.

Office hours at headquarters were a puzzle. Officially, work
began at half-past seven, but we often left by jeep from Tada

House after that time. When no field trips were planned for the afternoon, we departed for Tada House for lunch sometimes as early as noon and worked no more that day. On September 18, our work hours were lengthened to 8:30 to 4:30, with one and one-quarter hours for lunch, a schedule that improved the next day when lunch was delivered from Tada House to the office and we ate there. In spite of my frustration with the slow pace, I noted in my journal: "I believe this will be a good introduction to my work to be here for a few weeks."

The CI&E section, of which I was now a part, worked with the Japanese in all phases of information and education. Although at the regional level my responsibilities were then only with women's activities, I was glad to have glimpses while in Toku-shima of many facets of education and thus widen my experi-ences. I immediately began to appreciate the helpfulness of the first two Japanese women I got to know. On my first visit to the CI&E office, I met Miss Midori Bando, called Annie by everyone. She was a *nisei* (born in America to Japanese parents) born in Brighton, Colorado, and educated there in an elementary school before the family returned to Japan. Her Japanese was fluent, and her written and spoken English excellent. She was then interpreter for the major and, soon afterward, for me. When she interpreted, I always felt very secure about how my words were expressed in Japanese. She became one of my best friends on Shikoku. Early on, I also became well acquainted with Mrs. Harue Kushi, the staff member responsible for women's affairs in the prefectural government's social education section. She often accompanied Annie and me when we visited organizations. Both women gave generously of their time, Annie often interpreting on Sundays and half-day holidays, for example, when meetings were scheduled for times during which no other interpreter on the team was working. Fortunate indeed were the women of Tokushima Prefecture that Annie and Mrs. Kushi were involved during the early days of the occupation, when women were beginning to learn about and move toward their rightful places in society.

All of our field trips were made by jeep, driven very slowly because of unpaved, bumpy roads that were constantly being repaired. Since there was no machinery for road repair, the workers' efforts consisted simply of moving gravel from the sides of the road back into holes. Jeep riding was not comfortable. The driver and passenger in the front seat always felt jounced, and those in the back suffered even more. When we drove through towns and villages, where roads were better, drivers were tempted to increase speed. On one trip when the Japanese driver did just that, I thought, "We are really making time here"—until I looked at the speedometer and read ten miles an hour. Drivers always needed to be cautious in towns, however, because people walked freely in the streets and children played there.

Almost immediately, I began to accompany the major on field trips, and before long, I was taking my own. A situation arose on the first trip with the major that I was to encounter many times. It distressed me partly because it was wrong and partly because I did not know what to do about it. In Nagoya, we had been well aware that Japanese food was scarce, and we did not question why one of the occupation rules was that Americans should not consume it. Soon I learned another reason for American abstinence: if Japanese government officials entertained members of the occupation, the cost of the food and drink for all could be paid by public funds—in our case, from those budgeted for education. My concern, then, was not just with breaking the rules; my principles dictated that I could not eat food that was scarce to begin with and then have it subsidized by money intended for education. The major, however, seemed to have no such scruples: he ate with great relish all food set before him. I was always upset when I saw that a meal was prepared for us; whether my refusal to eat bothered him I never knew. When I was alone, the problem did not arise, because I carried rations or a sandwich and a thermos bottle of coffee from the mess hall.

During my ten weeks in Tokushima, I recorded estimates of the people present at a variety of gatherings. A summary of those—some of which I attended with the major and some without—now astonishes me. There were two meetings about citizens' public halls, with a total attendance of 800; fourteen meetings related to social education, attendance 2,675; four meetings with teachers, attendance 400; thirteen meetings with women's organizations, attendance 2,550; and four meetings with youth associations, attendance 700. The total of more than seven thousand people at thirty-seven meetings now seems large, and perhaps my estimates were high. Attendance levels, nevertheless, certainly demonstrated the eagerness of the people to become informed. Their interest was undoubtedly augmented by curiosity about Americans—and especially about the American woman working on the island.

As we began to hold meetings, I came face to face with the challenges I was up against. At Hisakatsu, perhaps six hundred women and men gathered at the school, counting all those looking in the windows, with most of the people sitting on the floor. The major spoke first, discussing democratic government; then I talked about democracy in the home. When I told a story of how my brother and I did the dishes together when children, Annie asked if he was my elder or younger brother. The point seemed irrelevant until she said there was no word for brother or sister—only for elder and younger brother or sister. At the close of the meeting, Annie and I were taken to an adjoining room for tea, along with the major and a woman official from the prefecture. The major first made sure we three women were seated. The Japanese men, as I recorded in my journal, then tried to make the same gesture: "When two women came into the room . . . , two men got up and offered their chairs, since all chairs were filled. And the women would not sit down. So finally the men rather sheepishly slipped back into their seats."

In social education meetings with both women and men in attendance, men asked almost all questions while women sat generally silent. Two random questions at one such gathering— one from a woman and one from a man—were revealing. The woman asked, "Are there men in the United States who, because they earn the money, feel they are entitled to run everything?" The man's question was "How can women take part in social education when farm women work all day in the fields and have to take care of the home and children, too?"

In Uchimachi, Annie and I met female teachers and a few male principals interested in homemaking. The teachers reported they were experiencing difficulties in teaching cooking and sewing to boys, along with the girls, in the fifth and sixth grades. This was not surprising, considering that men were not accustomed to helping in the home. When we were invited for tea after the meeting, the only ones included were the men principals; the women who conducted the program joined us only after I asked for them.

At seinendan (youth association) meetings, young women displayed the same reticence in the company of men as their elder counterparts. In Yokose, where about a third of the attendees, aged fifteen to twenty-five, were women, they sat together on one side of the room and said not a word. Although more young women than men were present at a gathering in Sanagawaki, they too were silent. But when Annie and I met a month later in Kawauchi with a reading club, we found young women more talkative, one even inquiring about educational opportunities for farm girls in the United States. A young man asked what kind of a husband I wanted. I wonder what I told him. Perhaps I prompted his question because I always tried to make my status as a single woman clear. The first reason was to obviate any misunderstanding of my status in the group: when the major and I had both spoken at earlier meetings, people had assumed I was his wife. The more serious reason grew out of experience as I learned that marriage was still of primary importance in Japanese society and was greatly sought after by most young women. What I said many times then was "if I had a husband, I would not be here." I learned later that all American women on the occupation staff were single.

During this time in Tokushima, I began to attend meetings of women's groups—by chance, a good cross-section: leaders from the prefecture, a city women's club, a town association, village organizations, a small group of businesswomen, and *fujinkai* (organizations composed primarily of housewives). Some aspect of each raised an issue, noted parenthetically below, that helped me identify points for my later training programs:

• When the president of the Tokushima Women's Club invited me to address the club, I asked her what my subject should be. My journal records that "she said, 'Happiness.' What a subject! So I hedged by saying that it might be more helpful if I talked about women's organizations. I mentioned as a possible subject the making of motions. Her face was blank—I felt she had no idea of what I meant." (*Note*: Parliamentary procedure needs explanation.)

• At a meeting of what seemed to be the twenty leading women for the prefecture-wide meeting, "One smoked. That's the first time I've seen that in a women's group." After the subject of finances was raised, one asked "how farmers' wives could get money for a club if their husbands are not willing to give them the money." (*Note*: Finances are a problem.)

• The town of Ko was our destination on Sunday afternoon only five days after my arrival in Tokushima. "The headman (mayor) was present as one of six men. The *fujinkai* president was a doctor, one of the few dressed in kimono on the hot day, and the vice president was wife of a Buddhist priest. . . . After the meeting, some came to talk to us. The 'freedom' [of democracy] seems to bother them. One said the children wouldn't do as they were told because they were free. Another asked advice about a widow who was taking up with a married man with a family because of the freedom. Golly! One has to be a Solomon! I did say that we have responsibilities still in democracy. Right is still right and wrong is still wrong." (*Note*: Do not try to give advice about Japanese customs that I don't understand.)

• At Ichijyo, I was the first American woman to visit the town: "We were at a meeting of all the women of Ichijyo—about three hundred crowded into a small hall on the school premises. . . . The headman was the chairman, with half a dozen men to support him from the place of honor in front. The women in charge were just a part of the audience and received no recognition at all. . . . After the meeting, thirteen of us were at lunch with not a woman present from the *fujinkai*. . . . [At the meeting,] I talked about equality in the home. . . . I got applause when I suggested that, by sharing responsibility in the home, the women would have time to attend meetings such as this." (*Note*: Women, not men, should conduct meetings.)

• The meeting in Kawashima, a joint gathering of the parent-teacher association (PTA) and *fujinkai* plus what seemed millions of children, was addressed by the team's officer for public health as well as the major and me, with a program of songs and dances by the children preceding the oratory. "I still feel that most *fujinkai* do not know how to organize or run their associations. A training class for presidents seems to me the next step. I shall try that when I get on my own." (*Note*: Leaders can be reached first.)

• Because of jeep trouble, the major, Annie, and I arrived late at Matsushige. After speaking, we retired for tea and soon collected twenty-five to thirty people: "All the talking was done by the major and the principal (male). We go to help the women, so the men monopolize the time. I'd kick 'em all out!" (*Note*: At this time, men should not attend women's groups.)

• Sutherland, a GI, drove Annie and me through lovely country on the ride of some one and a half hours to Hayashi. Several hundred people were present for the meeting presumably of the *fujinkai* that "turned out to be for practically everyone— women, a few men, and millions of children. The president spoke first, and no one seemed to listen. Then it was our turn, and the children trooped in from outside, too, to look and listen. . . . While we were speaking, Sutherland drove by on the road in the jeep. The children all thought he was coming into the yard— so all trooped out. Then, when he didn't stop, back in they came. This procedure happened again when he came back once more and stopped. . . . At one point, two men came in—sat down—decided it wasn't worth it—and walked out. . . . The whole affair was really very funny. But it also was very hard to talk with all those interruptions. I felt particularly sorry for Annie. . . . This *fujinkai* has 700 members but no regular meetings. And I'll bet a cookie no one elected the officers." (*Note*: A planned program is important. Organization constitutions must specify that officers are elected by majority vote.)

• At the first of three short sessions held with young women employees of the technical college, twelve attended—"all seated primly around the table, with hands folded in laps. They sat so quietly. [After I talked,] one asked how they could further educate themselves." At the other two meetings, we discussed the possibility of organizing a group to study whatever interested them. (*Note*: Small groups can be formed around interests.)

These contacts—no matter how brief—with hundreds of women of many backgrounds were valuable for the information I gathered and impressions I received. Surely, I thought, women in Ehime, Kochi, and Kagawa prefectures would be like those in Tokushima. If ten weeks in one prefecture permitted haphazard meetings with two thousand women, the prospects of reaching perhaps a million seemed less impossible.

Because I was eager to become as well informed as possible about education in Japan, I welcomed my few meetings with students. At one, when a group from the normal school visited the office, a young woman commented that "she thought girls should learn how to cook, sew, etc., and was disturbed because less time is being given to those subjects and more to other subjects." This comment was not surprising—but was a little distressing nevertheless. True, if patterns of the past continued, young women needed education only to become wives and mothers. But if women were ever to assume roles comparable to those of men, then they needed education to prepare themselves for their changed status.

One Sunday morning, the major and I were judges—along with two Japanese men—of a prefecture-wide oratorical contest featuring speeches in English, and I got a good demonstration of the unequal positions accorded school-age girls and boys. Most of the presentations by the thirteen boys and nine girls were shorter than the specified seven minutes. I described it in my journal:

> The English was better than I had anticipated. There were only a couple that I could barely understand. The girls had high-pitched voices on the whole [by custom] and suffered in that respect in comparison with the boys. Most were rather stiff, very few used gestures, some had papers. All but one girl spoke loud enough to be heard easily.
>
> One boy and one girl tied for first place, two boys tied for second, and a boy in fifth. The major suggested we have two firsts. . . . At that, a man suggested the boy be given first and the girl second. The major and I both blew our stacks at that! Why be unfair at the expense of the girl? It finally ended as the major had suggested.

Looking back now, I think such a dilemma probably would never have occurred under usual Japanese procedures at the time. The judges would privately have reached a consensus and declared the boy the winner.

When I finally returned to Takamatsu on November 4, Fred Kerlinger met me with a jeep and the news, by now not unexpected, that my quarters were not yet ready. I was to stay for a few days with Fred and his wife, Betty, who was employed at the team headquarters. After we left my luggage at their house, we drove to regional headquarters where I reported to the commanding officer — Colonel Robert E. Coughlin, one of the finest men I have ever known and a great talker. I always wondered if he realized that when I visited his office, I customarily arrived shortly before either lunch or dinner so our meetings could be terminated by my plea that "I must get to the mess hall before it closes."

When Betty and Fred took me to their guest room, they apologized for a problem they had been unable to resolve with the supply officer: a single mattress lay forlornly on a double bedspring. Another inconvenience: baths had to be taken soon after dinner because water was turned off at nine o'clock as a matter of conservation and was not available again until morning.

On my walk to the office the following morning, I tried to orient myself. The Kerlingers lived in a group of new dependent houses within the walls of Tamamo Castle. Once a "castle-on-a-plain" built in 1588 had stood there, so called because it was not on a high elevation like most castles. Although some of the watchtowers remained, nothing was left of the old building. The large house now called Tamamo Castle, built in 1914 by Lord Matsudaira of an old feudal family, was occupied by Colonel and Mrs. Coughlin. The sprawling house of some thirty rooms, single-storied except for one two-story wing, was built around four inner gardens and surrounded on three sides by outer gardens. Within the castle walls but in the opposite direction, another group of houses was being built.

On a Saturday morning a few days later, I moved to one of those houses—House 14. Downstairs were a living room, kitchen, closet, lavatory, and a room suitable for a dining room or bedroom. Upstairs were a good-sized bedroom with closet, small bedroom, hall closet, and bathroom. I decided, as the first resident, to occupy the larger bedroom. The supply section had sent a double mattress with a set of single bed springs, a pillow, sideboard, end table, full-length mirror, broken ironing board, two table lamps without bulbs, and twenty-five wooden hangers. Missing were chairs, bedding, toilet tissue, and cleaning supplies. In the bathroom, the tub was unpainted gray metal but usable. When I turned on the shower, water spurted all over because the head was not connected properly. The window was of clear glass and had no curtain, so I frosted the lower pane by rubbing it with a bar of soap. I did nothing about the upper pane, deciding that, if anyone wanted to look in badly enough to climb a nearby tree, he deserved to see something.

Somehow things got straightened out. I traded my double mattress for Betty's single one. After a call to the supply section, four wooden folding chairs, toilet tissue, a pail, and a Japanese twig broom arrived before I left for lunch. Since I had eaten my meals up to this time with Betty and Fred, I did not know the exact lunch hour at the mess hall, so my woes were compounded when I arrived after lunch had been served. I expressed proper repentance to the mess sergeant and was given, perhaps fittingly, a bologna sandwich. Then I saw the duty officer about sheets and blankets, only to be told, "We're not required to furnish sheets to civilians." No record appears in my journal of exactly what transpired next, but I remember that I lost my temper. And I slept that night with sheets on the bed.

Because the following day was Sunday, a day off, I could concentrate on settling in. As the workmen were all around fixing other houses, some problems were solved rather easily, sometimes with the help of the Japanese man in charge, who understood English quite well and could usually be found in a small building called "Office of the Actual Place of Liaison Section." Other household problems were harder to fix. The frequent failures of electric heaters and the hot-water heater were undoubtedly due to the inferior material available for manufacture and repair. Because spare parts were not standardized, a defective thermostat on a hot-water heater, for example, was finally replaced by a new one made to fit only that heater. During the cold winter months, we often lacked a uniform supply of heat and hot water. One night after dinner, the water heater was so hot that only steam and water the color of root beer came out when a faucet was opened. Really serious trouble occurred once when I noticed fecal matter in the water, and we had to boil water for several days. But after a large tank was erected on the grounds to supply clean water to the castle and dependent houses, most of those problems were eliminated.

Not all our domestic problems were serious, however. Once I requested the assistance of a carpenter at the "Office of the Actual Place" after discovering large, open spaces around pipes under the kitchen sink. Perhaps my pronunciation of *nezumi* had a Nagoya accent—at any rate, the carpenter simply looked puzzled. Only after I drew a picture of an animal with large ears and a long tail did he laughingly recognize my rat.

Two weeks after I reached Takamatsu, the adjutant asked if I would take care of Stella Hoshimiya, a secretary just arrived from Tokyo. Stella, a *nisei* from California, took the second bedroom upstairs. Although she disclaimed fluency in Japanese, her language ability often helped us. We would never have gotten a stand put on our small Christmas tree, for instance, without her directions to the five men assigned to the project. Stella christened our house the "BWQ"—bachelor women's quarters—and we were later joined at separate times by a female captain and a public health nurse. By that time, we knew we soon were to move to the castle because our house was needed for dependent housing.

On May 1, 1948, we were moved to Wing G (for "girls") of Tamamo Castle, a typical Japanese setting but with Western conveniences added. The colonel assigned us to adjoining rooms. Mine was a ten-mat room, measuring about twelve feet by eighteen, as compared with the other two eight-mat rooms. Our rooms were equipped comfortably with furniture left by BCOF after the withdrawal of its troops; the feet of all pieces were mounted on thin strips of wood to protect the *tatami*.

Only infrequently did cool breezes ever find their way into our rooms during the stifling, humid days of summer. In the first year, mosquitoes made our nights miserable because, although we smeared on repellent before going to bed, it always wore off during the night. In the winter, cold blasts off the Inland Sea turned our corridors into wind tunnels and slipped around our paper doors. When we had moved from House 14, I was instructed not to take the electric heaters. But that first winter we were grateful that I had disobeyed those orders, because the four heaters provided us with one for each bedroom and one for the bathroom. After having taken such a long time to get settled, I then lived in the castle for the balance of my stay on Shikoku.

Settling into the Takamatsu office proved considerably easier than getting settled into a house had been—and involved fewer changes over time. During my time on Shikoku from August 1947 to February 1951, Fred and his successor, Robert M. Hager, were section chiefs. Bernard J. Dobbins (known as Dobbie) was the Kagawa team officer until the teams were abolished late in 1949; then he joined the regional staff as youth affairs officer after home leave. Working with Fred and me were a large number of Japanese staff members—sixteen, for instance, in November 1949. All contributed to the work of the office, serving as interpreters, translators, historians, scholars, typists, artists, and assistants in women's and youth affairs.

I soon learned how fortunate I was to work with a good section chief who always encouraged my efforts. Fred was quick and energetic, with a fine mind. Trained in an Army language school to speak and read Japanese, he was also caring in his relations with people. His often excitable and sometimes even explosive way of speaking belied a heart as soft as a marshmallow.

Education was a key aspect of the postwar reforms, and in the parallel occupation structure, positions like Fred's were the linchpin between the civil education branch of the Allied military government and the education branch of the Japanese government. The new educational policy—set on the national level by the Japanese Ministry of Education under direction of CI&E, SCAP—involved comprehensive changes in curriculum, textbooks, buildings, and teachers and their training. Directives were sent down from the ministry to the prefectures for implementation. American civil education officers in military government units then assisted Japanese officials at lower levels in carrying out those policies. Similar procedures were followed for social education programs, which included adult education, libraries, and organizations for women, youth, and parents and teachers. When officers assigned exclusively to women's affairs were added to civil education sections, the importance attached to the women of Japan in the reform process seemed clear.

TOP: *My English class for industrial officials in Nagoya, December 1946. At far left is Mr. Kyo Funaki (my star pupil). Seated to my left is Mr. Kenji Sasaki, my instructor at the Air Force language school and the interpreter for these classes.* LEFT: *Mrs. Kyoko Nakano and her son, 1946–47. Mrs. Nakano was the interpreter at the Chiyoda Hotel in Nagoya; her father was Mr. Kenji Sasaki.* BOTTOM: *Annie Bando and me at Ikeda, November 1947.*

TOP: *"Office of the Actual Place,"* our liaison for housing matters while living in House 14, 1947–48. LEFT: *Stella Hoshimiya and me on our bicycles, February 1948.* BOTTOM: *In the Tamamo Castle grounds, December 1947. These three photos were taken in Takamatsu.*

TOP: *Girl Scout Troop 1 in Kochi, June 1948.* RIGHT: *Our train car, The Eagle, and the young Japanese man who prepared our meals on board. Photo taken October 1949.* BOTTOM: *Women from civil and social education sections of the four prefectures in January 1948. Miss Harada, who interpreted for me for a short time before returning to her teaching job, is directly below me at left. Miss Masaki, who provided us with ice at one meeting, is in the middle wearing glasses. Behind her, partially obscured, is Mrs. Inagaki; to her left, on the end, is Mrs. Kushi. Both of the latter women appear often in the book.*

A press photo of me, taken in 1948.

Japanese members of the Takamatsu office staff. At the far left, wearing a kimono, is Mrs. Imamura, the first of the "four women" in chapter 8. Kneeling in the front row is Mrs. Seno, the second of the "four women." Miss Matsumura, my primary interpreter and the third of the "four women," is standing on the far right of the middle row. In the middle of that row is Mrs. Hayashi, my assistant who had such difficulty keeping her little boy; she is the fourth of the "four women." Mr. Wada, who met with the emperor, is on the back row, far right. Kneeling in the front row at the far right is the artist who made the posters I used in training sessions.

Left to right: Bernard J. Dobbins ("Dobbie"), me, Lt. Leland Daly, Betty Kerlinger, Fred Kerlinger. Photo taken in November 1949.

At a hotel in the San Francisco airport on my way to Japan in 1993.

TOP: *Toshio Watanabe took me to meet his parents at their home in Osaka, May 1993.* LEFT: *Kyo Funaki, my star pupil from my English class in 1946, came to see me during my 1993 visit to Japan.* BOTTOM: *While in Japan in May 1993, I was delighted to see Yuka Moriguchi Tsuchiya, who had interviewed me in 1978 for her graduate work at the University of Maryland.*

To my right is Mr. Tada, who graciously entertained us at Tada House during my trip to Japan in May 1995. To my left is Hiroko Kondo, who interpreted for me during much of my visit. Her mother was Mrs. Harue Kushi, who had been the prefectural official who worked with women during the occupation years—and my good friend.

A highlight of the May 1995 trip was the time I got to spend with my long-time friend, Annie Bando Sakai.

During my May 1995 trip, a group of women on Shikoku—some of whom remembered me from the occupation—told me what they had been doing with women's issues since my time there.

In recognition of my starting the Girl Scouts on Shikoku in the late 1940s, the current organization honored me during my 1995 visit at a special event with tea, flowers, and demonstrations. These girls are performing the Awa Odori, a traditional dance.

5 · · ·

Wave-Rings

in the Water

Soon after my arrival in Takamatsu, I began discussing with Fred how I might best approach my responsibilities as women's affairs officer. I believed if women were to be reached through *fujinkai*, then they first had to learn how to conduct the business of those organizations democratically. From my experience in Tokushima, I felt sure that no one—government officials, leaders of associations, or members—really knew how to do that. So when, ten days after my arrival in Takamatsu, an editorial entitled "The Technique of Democracy" appeared in the *Nippon Times*, Fred and I were delighted that the eminent English-language journal devoted so much space to the subject uppermost in our minds. Because it so clearly summarizes the situation, I will quote extensively from it here:

> Although there may still be some skepticism abroad, there can no longer be anyone in close touch with Japanese conditions who has the slightest doubt about the sincere desire of the overwhelming majority of the Japanese to embrace democracy. But a desire for democracy, however sincere and fervent, and a successful practice of democracy are

two very different things. Possession of the former by no means assures the automatic attainment of the latter. . . .

It is, therefore, highly welcome that we are beginning to give considerable heed to the problem of propagating proper rules of order in the conduct of business in various clubs and organizations formed among the people. . . . If popular organizations among the people, such as women's clubs, parent-teacher associations, labor unions, farmers' cooperatives, and the like, can be made to function efficiently through democratic procedure in the conduct of their meetings, the people will come to have faith in democratic methods and they will also gain the experience to make their political and governmental institutions function democratically. . . .

How truly this is no exaggeration can readily be appreciated by those who have seen many Japanese organizations carry on their meetings. So lacking in knowledge of the technique of self-governing procedure are most Japanese, accustomed for ages to simply obeying directions from above, that they flounder pathetically when no one individual assumes sole command. Even in meetings of intelligent men with definite ideas, there is usually surprising inability to get any practical business done. Either there is interminable talk which never resolves itself into a practical decision, or the group defers to the domination of one individual.

The situation is made worse by the common Japanese misconception that democratic methods mean heckling and disorder and intransigence of minority groups. . . . Under democratic procedure there is no need for such practices, for everyone is assured of a fair chance to be heard, and resort to such obtrusive practices merely obstructs the ends of the meeting and impairs its efficiency. . . .

. . . Having had no opportunity to see other examples,

the Japanese people generally fail to realize how sadly lacking they are in the knowledge of [the] technique [of handling meetings]. . . . The work of education along this line,
highly limited in scope though it may seem, is actually sur-
prisingly germane to the future of democracy in general in
Japan and deserves the unreserved support of all those
enlightened enough to appreciate its value.

Although Fred and I knew that only a small number of Japanese citizens would read this editorial, we felt that well-educated
and active leaders would be most likely to do so. The newspaper
clearly articulated the task facing us.

About a week later, a press release from the Shikoku Military
Government Region appeared in all Shikoku newspapers, explaining my position in this effort to foster democratic organizations. It read in part:

Now attached to the staff of the Shikoku Military Government Region is Miss Carmen Johnson, whose principal
work will be with women's activities and women's organizations on Shikoku Island. . . . [She] will try to show
women . . . how to form democratic organizations, what
activities are worthwhile for democratic organizations,
how to elect officers, how to make a motion, etc. . . . She
will work very closely and intimately with Shikoku
women to teach them their rights and how to exercise
these rights.

Ten days later at a meeting in Takamatsu of Shikoku civil education officers, I spent the thirty minutes assigned to me in out-
lining some tentative plans, based on my experiences in Tokushima Prefecture. I reported a major problem in my journal: "I
met opposition when I said no men were to be at the meetings.
I asked them who they thought we were trying to help—the
women, or the men who had no business there. This idea of

[their] not wanting to hurt the feelings of the men makes me mad."

My next step was to ask *fujinkai* to complete by December 31, 1947, a survey composed in the civil education office. Although I already had many ideas in mind, feedback from the women's groups themselves would help to confirm or challenge my suppositions.

Then, on November 29, I went to a three-day conference for twenty-five women's affairs officers at Eighth Army headquarters in Yokohama, at which the future scope of women's affairs officers' work was discussed. On the first morning, group meetings were led by two women from CI&E, SCAP. In the afternoon, we met Japanese women leaders, all but one educated in the United States and speaking English. The next day, my journal records that

> the morning was spent in discussions of labor problems and public health. . . . Also had a speech by Mrs. Yamakawa, chief of the Women's and Minors' Bureau, Labor Ministry. She holds the highest position of any woman in the Japanese government. Yet she is the plainest looking soul. I could hardly hear her voice when she was talking. I contrasted her to our women high in government. Guess that told me we cannot judge Japanese women by our standards.

The afternoon was spent on reports about public welfare and youth organizations. The conference ended the next morning with two major suggestions for our work: we were to begin to work with women in their organizations already in existence and to encourage those associations to be independent of governmental control. In the afternoon, we went to Tokyo to the Diet building, "quite handsome [but with] no heat and very little light. I was terribly interested. We met most of the women members. I was much impressed by Mrs. Shidzue Kato, formerly Baroness

Ishimoto, 'the Margaret Sanger of Japan.' On the whole, I would say the women were a most impressive lot."

One of the first requests I had made when arriving in Takamatsu was for an interpreter. By January 1948, only a month before my meetings were to begin with women in the four prefectures, I still had no prospects. The difficulty arose partly because my requirements limited the number of candidates. First, I required the interpreter to be a woman, for I felt strongly that an American woman should use a Japanese woman to speak for her. In practical terms, a woman was usually a better interpreter than a man because she interpreted accurately even though she might not agree with what was said; she was more conscientious and therefore more accurate; if she did not understand the speaker's meaning, she was more apt to ask for clarification; and when interpreting for a woman, she may have felt more at ease with the speaker. The second requirement was that she be able to travel throughout the island and be willing to stay by herself in inns on field trips. Third, although her English need not be as fluent as that of Annie Bando in Tokushima, she must understand the language well enough to put my words into Japanese when we addressed a large audience or held a meeting.

Finally, the executive officer for the region requested that Miss Harada, a young *nisei* from another prefecture, be relieved of her duties as a teacher to accompany me on trips planned for February. Fred found a place for her to live in Takamatsu, and I eagerly awaited her arrival on February 2—the day before meetings were scheduled in Kagawa Prefecture. When she arrived accompanied by her mother, I was a little surprised but pleased that I could tell them how glad I was that such a good interpreter could help me. I assured both that I would try very hard to make the experience pleasant for Miss Harada.

After the first day we worked together, I commented in my journal that she "does very well. She's quick and catches on admirably." However, from the very beginning she kept "talking about [working only] a month," so my hopes for having her stay with me permanently were not high. Nonetheless, I tried to make the trips as comfortable as possible and probably succeeded except on two occasions. In one city after we finally got her settled at her inn, she telephoned to my billet to say she could not get anything to eat because she had not brought rice. The civil education officer solved that problem by having her join the team interpreters for meals. Another unusual occurrence did not seem to bother her, unexpected as it was. To reach Matsuyama from Takamatsu, we rode in the special coach, The Eagle, accompanied by three American women from Tokyo also with the occupation. We went to the station considerably earlier than the departure time of 11:30 p.m. The other women were in bed, and Miss Harada and I were undressing when the door was flung open, and three Japanese men rushed in to bid one of the women good-bye. Sitting up in bed, she calmly accepted their thanks and good wishes as Miss Harada and I stood by, dressed only in our slips. We exchanged bows with the three men as they withdrew.

On those February trips, the last city Miss Harada and I visited was her home, so she remained there when I returned to Takamatsu. She was having trouble making up her mind about taking on the job permanently, but she did say she would talk it over with her mother. On Monday, she was not at the office, so I presumed that she had decided not to join the staff. Then, on the following day, I received a letter explaining her decision:

> As you probably know, in Japan it is the custom for every girl to marry. Another thing, which I presume you already know, is that in Japan it is the custom for a "go-between" and the parents to decide the marriage. Since these are the customs of Japan, I living in Japan must also follow these customs.
>
> Now in Japan the public has more respect and thinks

more of a person who is a teacher than one who may be in Kochi one day and in Takamatsu the next. Naturally the teacher will be more domestic as she will, after school, have more time at home and will learn the different household tasks to be able to make a home of her own when the time comes. At least, the public, the people, will think that she will be more capable than a person who is never at home.

Being that I live in Japan and because my parents are constantly worrying about getting me settled, I feel it is my duty that I should do what a Japanese girl should do.

I interviewed five more women who spoke English, but none met all the qualifications for interpreter. Over the months while the search continued, women on the teams interpreted during field trips. Then Miss Yoriko Matsumura, a friend of Mrs. Sumiko Hayashi—my assistant in the regional civil education office—came to apply for the position. I hired her immediately, and she stayed with me until my departure in 1951.

Plans were modest for my first meetings in the prefectures in December 1947 and January 1948 because I had no interpreter, the personnel and settings were unknown in all prefectures except Tokushima, and the results of the survey of *fujinkai* were not yet available. Customarily, requests for meetings with groups and for conferences with individuals went from the regional office to the team, where the civil education officer then turned to Japanese officials to make final arrangements. Although my request was for "a small, selected *fujinkai*," the groups with which I met were very different from what I'd requested. I don't know whether that was because of a lack of clarity in my requests, misunderstanding by the team officers, or confusion on the part of Japanese officials. In fact, my plans for meetings in all four prefectures throughout the years were almost never carried out as

I'd anticipated. I soon learned to talk on any subject to whoever arrived, whether or not they were the ones expected. I also soon learned to adapt my living habits to accommodations provided by the three teams I visited (in Kagawa Prefecture, of course, I stayed in my own room in Takamatsu). Because living quarters at the teams were limited for visitors, especially for a female, I never knew from trip to trip just where I might be sent. Sometimes I was given a room in the BOQ; sometimes, in the home of an American family; sometimes, in an unoccupied dependent house. I preferred a BOQ room, for there I could be independent to carry out my schedules and could share rides with team officers to and from the mess hall. Although families were always cordial, staying in someone's home seemed to me an imposition.

On my first field trips with Miss Harada, I focused on the election of officers and voting. I knew that men were usually presidents of *fujinkai*, so I felt that electing women to that position should be the first priority. Mr. Iwasaki, the office artist, made six posters related to the nomination and election of officers, all six large enough to be seen across a meeting room.

In Kagawa Prefecture at the very first conference, the existence of a government federation became apparent, even though government control of organizations was supposed to have been abolished under the new constitution. Then came the meeting with the women's "cultural club." My journal notes that we had about "sixty women. Spoke about election of officers, aided by six large posters. . . . Then I met with the officers for a few minutes."

Matsuyama provided a particular surprise when the meeting we had requested for a small group materialized into a gathering of eight hundred women.

First thing I noticed were some men. While we [the interpreter and I] were wondering what we should do, the woman chairman asked them to leave. Soon most of them had gone; eventually all. . . . Women kept coming and coming. Soon some mats were unrolled in front for them to sit on. The last arrivals got there at eleven o'clock— the meeting started at nine-thirty. In introductory re- marks, the chairman said it was the first time there had ever been a meeting of women without the men there. She thanked me for that.

In the afternoon I brought up subjects of [the undesir- ability of] having only one meeting a year and of having huge organizations with small attendance. That was quite a shock [to them]! . . .

Later at a meeting with the head of the prefectural social education section, he told me it was the first time there had been a meeting without men. He said he was worried. I told him he need not have been as the women did beautifully.

On this trip to Matsuyama, I was made aware for the first time of a customary Japanese courtesy—meeting visitors upon arrival and seeing them off upon departure. Three women were with the CI&E officer at the train the afternoon I arrived, and six were at the station at nine on the morning I left. Because I expected to arrive and depart often and because I knew the dif- ficulties involved in travel, I expressed my thanks that morning for their courtesy but asked them please not to do it again. After this same little speech was repeated on enough trips throughout the island, word got around that saved women making long and what seemed to me unnecessary trips at all hours of the day and night.

The town of Naruto in Tokushima Prefecture was the scene of the final meeting in this first series. There the "small group" numbered about five hundred, including some high school girls, a male teacher, and several other men who occupied chairs while women stood. When I announced that we would ask the men to leave before the question period, to my surprise they got up and left. The noise of children running through the halls distressed me because Annie (who was then interpreting for me) had trouble hearing over the racket. After we spoke, we asked for questions: "Not a question. That always amazes me."

During the same two months that those initial meetings were held, one day I had some visitors at the office:

> Two women from the Kagawa prefectural federation came to see me. They know I don't approve of federations, but they want to tell me all about it. The prefecture started it, but they have now broken away. If true, wonderful! I told them there needs to be a more democratic constitution for the organizations, at least.

I also had a visit from Mrs. Hoshi, president of the *fujinkai* in a nearby city. "Just as I suspect 100 out of 100 other organizations are handled, the vote of the members is not taken when decisions are made. She is at a loss as how to handle 800 members. I learned she is from Tokyo and probably resented by the local ladies. I recommended starting from scratch and including only those people interested in an organization run democratically. If she had 50 interested women, she could make a go of it." About a month later, "while I was in Tokushima, something happened that certainly is gratifying. Mrs. Hoshi called to see if I was in. She came to Takamatsu to tell the prefectural people that her *fujinkai* was not joining the federation because they weren't ready. I can hardly believe it. I talked to her only once but maybe that stuck. Guess I won't pack my trunk yet."

In February 1948, I began the ambitious program of training leaders of *fujinkai*, who could then report back to their organizations and put the new theories into practice. In preparation for the sessions, the regional office issued a press release to stress two points—that individual associations should be functioning democratically before anyone began to think of forming federations and that the government should have no connection with women's organizations nor interfere in their activities. The press release, issued on February 6, read:

Miss Johnson, Women's Affairs Officer Shikoku Military Government Region, made the following statement, regarding women's organizations on Shikoku.

"During the past two months work has been begun by the Shikoku Military Government Region Women's Affairs Officer with women's organizations of Shikoku. Two trends have been noticed that are not in keeping with democratic principles.

"In the first place, the federation of women's organizations under the sponsorship of the prefectural officials is premature and unwise. Most individual associations need reorganization before they can function in a democratic manner. Only after all women's organizations are in good order individually will it be time to consider federation. That time may not be for months, or even years, to come.

"In the second place, there should be no government interference or connection with women's associations. These groups of women should join an association because they want to. They are not compelled to belong to any organization. These organizations should be independent and self-supporting. There is no reason why they should be under any influence whatsoever of any governmental officials. In a democratic country organizations have the privilege of criticizing the government instead of being run by the government.

"Two great needs in Shikoku today are the reorganization of women's associations along democratic lines and the education of women leaders in the ways this may be accomplished."

Two years later, I learned from Mrs. Hayashi that the words of that ordinary press release became known as "Jonson-san's *sengen*," or declaration. I was horrified, for I never intended to issue an edict to Japanese women. However, I must admit that considerable good probably came from it.

We selected parliamentary procedures as the theme for our first training sessions for leaders, but the problem was how to present concepts so strange to Japanese culture and practice. How could we make them understandable and meaningful? How could women visualize the steps taken to make a motion and vote? As a demonstration, I wrote a skit for fifteen participants and had it translated and duplicated so that each woman playing a role had a copy. Parts were then read at meetings, on the first day for two representatives invited from each *fujinkai* and on the second day for any interested other women; many attended both sessions. We again used the large posters about election of officers. To show that the military government supported the women's program, the commanding officer and the CI&E officer in each prefecture gave greetings at the opening of its conference.

In Kagawa, out of about two hundred,

I picked fifteen women at random and gave them copies of the skit to read. . . . The first time was not so good but the second good enough. A few ladies were slow in catching on—just like Americans would be. After the second time, the woman who was supposedly elected president made a little speech about trying to do her best. We all had lots of fun over it. And I think they learned something from it. . . .

[On the second day] the skit was very successful. One woman said that, after hearing the program yesterday and today, she began to understand what we were saying.

In Kochi Prefecture, about sixty women met in a girls' high school in what was apparently the library:

> Again, we had lots of fun with the skit. Highly successful. At the end of the meeting, I suggested we close by a motion for adjournment. We got the motion made but not seconded. So I stopped the chairman there. Then came discussion. One woman stood up and said, 'I think we should do it again.' Everyone just howled. So we did it again. I remarked to Miss Harada that I thought probably this was the first time the ladies had ever done that. She said it was probably the first time it had been done in Japan.

Whether her statement was true or not, it certainly gave me a boost.

The second day in Kochi attracted only about forty. When we got back to Takamatsu, we discovered that the conference had fallen during the celebration of the lunar new year, so women had probably chosen to spend the holiday with their families rather than learning democratic procedures.

Meetings on both days in Ehime were attended by about seven hundred: "Again the play went off very well. There were a few ladies who had memorized their parts. The closing was by adjournment after a motion was made. We had to do that three times before it was done anywhere near correctly. The chairman was really very good and self-possessed."

About one hundred fifty women attended the first session in Tokushima Prefecture, held in a primary school where "the wind whistled through the broken and missing glass windows." The team commanding officer and the major in CI&E spoke, followed by two men from the prefecture.

> We didn't even get started until almost eleven o'clock. Three men were in the audience in the morning; they were not there in the afternoon.

After lunch, we met in a smaller room so it was a little warmer. But the *tatami* necessitated no shoes. . . . Problem: when seated on the floor on *tatami*, does one stand to address the chair? What would Mr. Roberts suggest?

After the meeting adjourned, discussion was brought up about tea tomorrow. Mrs. Kushi [from the prefectural social education office] tried to have the decision made democratically [with a motion] and did right well after some help from us.

[On the following day] we had tea and little cakes after the meeting. They voted yesterday to do that. One woman made a long speech about how I took my shoes off on the *tatami*. Such a simple matter seemed so significant [to them]. . . .

Until women's affairs officers became assistant civil education officers in August 1948 and my title and responsibilities changed, I continued to hold periodic meetings with the leaders of *fujinkai* in the four prefectures. Many women attended regularly, often at great sacrifice. Even though the story of one leader in Kagawa Prefecture may be atypical, it illustrates the earnest desire of country women to learn about democracy and practice its principles.

A woman and her two daughters came to the office to see us. They live with thirty families on an island off Sakaide. Her husband is the headman. No electricity, no radios (no batteries to run them), no boat service, newspapers from Sakaide. Five islands form a village. From her island, she has to take a fishing boat to another island where the regular passenger boat stops.

The older women on the island cannot read. If girls finish girls' high school, they do not remain on the island. She wants to organize a *fujinkai*. Imagine trying to help her with the handicaps she will have. But she ought to be able to do something for the women.

This woman carried away the six large posters about nominating officers and voting that we used at the December meeting. When she returned for the May meeting, she brought them back with an apology for keeping them so long, but she said she had read them to the people on the island. For the six people there who could read, she took home with her copies of the only pamphlet then available about organizations. When she asked what to do when voting by ballot if they cannot read or write, I suggested using symbols for various people. There was no place on her island for a group to meet, as the school was running on a double shift, and there was no electricity to furnish light for evening meetings. I suggested that a project might be to teach the women to read and write.

At meetings during this time, we continued to talk about democratic principles for a *fujinkai*, practiced making motions and voting, and tried to add some new concept at each series. Because the first skit was so successful, I wrote another to illustrate principles of democratic procedures. In one series, when I was acting as chairman, Mrs. Hayashi was primed—unknown to anyone else—to vote against a motion, thereupon discrediting in Japanese eyes the leadership of the chairman. After I asked for and received a motion and second to adjourn the meeting, with no discussion following the motion, the members were asked to vote. "All those in favor, say 'yes'" brought forth a great chorus of affirmative votes. "All those opposed, say 'no.'" From someone (Mrs. Hayashi, of course) came a clear "no." A hush came over the audience, followed by an exchange of worried glances that someone had opposed the chairman. We hurriedly explained that even one person has the right to vote against a motion and a chairman, but I felt they were still uneasy about that obstinate woman who defied everyone by voting no.

Three incidents recorded in my journal about meetings held in 1948 indicated some issues that troubled women leaders. One was only a brief statement: "The question of getting women to speak and be active in organizations came up again." A second showed that many still sought direction from authority—a tendency complicated by the authority role played by the occupation. A group in Tokushima Prefecture was "trying to have voluntary membership with dues, but the women were not in accord. They want me to come and tell them [what to do]. I put the responsibility back on them." The third illustrated the continuing practice of direction by prefectural government officials in Kochi Prefecture: "We were talking about getting farm women interested in government, etc. I recommended attendance at meetings of farm cooperatives. The woman social education official said the prefectural section responsible for farm cooperatives was going to have half the officers women at the next election. Since when does government say who the officers will be!"

During 1948, the regional civil education staff produced several publications related to organizations: a sample constitution, a handbook for parent-teacher associations, and a book entitled *Techniques of Democracy* (Minshushugi no Gijutsu), a guide to procedures for Japanese organizations that Fred had written. Published in both Japanese and English with the Japanese situation in mind, this volume was used in all kinds of training courses and meetings. Some Japanese women, however, made negative comments about the book because it showed women in *mompe* and kimono but not in Western-style dress.

A more detailed survey of *fujinkai* in December 1948 revealed, disappointingly though not unexpectedly, that little change had occurred during the past year. Moreover, other problems appeared. One was that organizations were not holding regularly planned meetings. Some met only once a year and others not at all. I believed that little in the way of women's education was possible unless organizations had regular meetings with planned programs. The second was that, because the amount of dues was infinitesimal, little money was available for carrying on association business and programs. With the average yearly dues for Shikoku approximately ¥24 (about seven cents) a year, programs had to utilize only local people; experts could not be brought in at any great expense to the association. Another discovery about organization practices further complicated the problem of inadequate funds: "The treasurer is usually a wealthy person. Then if money is needed . . . the treasurer puts some in."

For the first few months of 1949, I continued the same schedule of talking to leaders, leaving to the judgment of the women themselves and to social education officials the question of who fit into that category. As might be expected, those who attended were principally older women. Many who were influential before and during the war simply continued to be so. Two meetings held with such leaders were of interest. In Kagawa Prefecture, members were to choose in a mock election a vice president to fill the place of one who had just resigned.

> Mrs. Inagaki [from the team civil education office] acting as chairman of the nominating committee suggested two names. Then we had one nomination from the floor. On the first ballot, the highest number of votes was three short of a majority, with the other two receiving six and seven votes. One other woman received a write-in vote. I explained that the ones with few votes could withdraw, but the president could not eliminate them. Or [a voter whose candidate was far behind] could say to herself that her candidate could not be elected anyway so she would vote for someone else. In any case, we had to vote again. Ballots were passed out, and the names written. Then up popped a minority candidate to withdraw her name. Immediately the other did also. That left the high woman

and the one write-in vote. So we had to collect the ballots
and write once more.

The second meeting took place on a very hot day in Ehime
Prefecture. Miss Masaki, the able prefectural women's affairs
official, was very clever in trying to make everyone comfortable
in the heat.

At our feet was a pan containing a small cake of ice. Then
a pail of small pieces was passed around in the audience.
Miss Matsumura [my interpreter] said the women would
feel it was impolite to eat the ice in front of me. So I told
them please do so. Then she prompted me to tell them to
use their folding fans if they wished, and I used my own. If
I had not told them to, it would have been impolite to fan.

During the same period we were meeting with the generally
older, established leaders, we also scheduled meetings to reach
younger women, whose modesty generally prevented them from
considering themselves possible leaders, so they did not want to
attend our leadership meetings. The attendance at these meetings with younger women ranged from two to eighty. Two questions concerned dues for a *fujinkai*:

Some of the women wanted to know how to raise money
for their organizations. I started to figure out how much
would come in from dues when I was stopped by the
remark that not all dues were collected. It finally came out
that the women could not get the ¥20 (about five cents)
for yearly dues from their husbands so preferred to earn
the money outside. Well!

Big to-do when I said drop those from the rolls who
were not interested [enough to attend meetings]. They
need their dues, they said. So I asked why pay any dues if
you do not attend. They murmured about its being a service to the organization. So I tried to explain the difference

between charity . . . where you probably expect no return
and payment of dues where you should expect something
in return.

The source of confusion on this issue, of course, was that the
payment of dues had been compulsory before and during the
war, with no expectation of the payer gaining any benefit per-
sonally, as the money was used for the war effort.

A third question, unrelated to *fujinkai*, was one I could not
begin to answer: "One wanted help about the cost of weddings.
Many parents of the bride cannot afford money for all the trap-
pings. So many divorces result because the bride has not brought
enough to her husband. This shows the feudalistic system still at
work in the country, at least, when the parents force young men
to divorce their wives against their will."

When the second *fujinkai* survey revealed the absence of planned
programs, I wrote a pamphlet entitled "Planning a Year's Program for an Organization" (Dantai no Ichinenkan no Purogu-
ramu Keikaku ni Tsuite). Miss Matsumura was to translate my
English version, and copies in Japanese would be offered to the
prefectural social education sections to reproduce and distribute
to any organization they felt could benefit from it. Contents
included the definition of a program and where it fit into the
order of business of a meeting; a step-by-step description of how
to use questionnaires to find subjects of interest to members; and
a list of suggested programs, month-by-month, for *fujin dantai*
(women's organizations in general), a PTA, and a *seinendan*, each
program followed by an explanation of the meetings. We discovered a problem in translating the activity suggested for the last
meeting: a picnic with children and husbands as guests. Mrs.
Hayashi, who was helping with the project, mentioned that no
commonly used word in Japanese was equivalent to "husband" in
the neutral sense Americans used it. "The Japanese word *dan-*

nasama means 'lord and master' in that connection," she said. I managed to restrain myself from commenting.

After a third survey of *fujinkai* in December 1949, some little progress was noted. Of the some eight hundred *fujinkai* reporting, 61 percent had a planned program for at least four meetings during the coming year. However, 144 *fujinkai* reported they accepted government subsidies, which were now illegal under the new social education law. This problem was, of course, included in planning for future meetings.

When the prefectural teams were closed in the fall of 1949, we regional officers assumed sole responsibility throughout the island for our assigned topical areas. Although my expanded responsibilities meant that I could devote less time to women's affairs, I continued to schedule as many meetings with *fujinkai* leaders and members as possible.

Early in January 1950, about fifty women gathered in the Kagawa prefectural building: "It was cold! Someone asked why there was no heat when there was a stove in the room. One woman replied that the men were still feudalistic and would not give us heat." Pretty funny, I thought. When I went to the regional building for lunch, I made arrangements to hold the afternoon meeting in the heated conference room there: "One remarked, 'We were in hell this morning. Now we are in heaven.' Hell in Japan must be cold." Recalling that about a year earlier women had asked that recreation be included in meetings, I suggested that we get warm before starting the afternoon session. I taught them a singing game from my Girl Scout days that guaranteed to raise their temperature. After we finished the game, we were all breathless and warm, ready to collapse in our chairs. And I will never forget the sight of a roomful of elderly, sedate women dressed in kimono bobbing up and down to a Girl Scout song.

During my time in Japan, events constantly reminded me of the challenges the Japanese faced in making a transition to democracy. On one trip on The Eagle when Mrs. Hayashi and I were traveling alone, at one point she got off the car to walk up the platform past the engine while the train stood at a station. The engineer asked her about the American woman riding in the special car, assuming that "she must be the wife of a very important man." He could not conceive of a woman having significance in her own right.

From the beginning, of course, I held to my firm position that the status of women was equal to that of men. Japanese men had been told over and over that the new constitution guaranteed equality and that we Americans thought women were their equals; but perhaps more important, our actions showed democracy was more than words. Because we felt women were capable of conducting the business of their *fujinkai* but were inhibited in the presence of men, we excluded men from our meetings. On the other hand, since men also needed help understanding the principles of democracy, we did not want what was discussed in training sessions to be kept secret from them. So from the early days of my work with women, I usually included in my final remarks words something like these, after making sure they realized I was not married:

> Now you know I am an *oludo missu* [old maid] so may wonder when I give you some advice about your husbands. We have talked today about many important new ideas. So tonight when you get home, fix up a very good dinner of things your husband especially likes and feed him well. Then when he is full of good food and relaxed, you tell him what we talked about today. Maybe you can help him understand that democracy should also be present at home now that the new constitution guarantees equal rights for women and men.

No doubt our insistence on democratic principles was not the only thing challenging for the Japanese. Even estimating the age of Americans was difficult. When women asked how old I was, in this country where age was venerated, I never hesitated to tell them, realizing that I might seem even younger than I was to hold a responsible position with the occupation. But I did not feel that way when men inquired about my age simply out of curiosity. After it happened for the umpteenth time, I said to Miss Matsumura, "The next time a man asks me how old I am just because he is inquisitive, I'm going to say ninety-five." I would never have given such an answer on Shikoku, where we were known. But once when Miss Matsumura, a friend, and I were on a holiday on Honshu Island traveling on a third-class train along the Sea of Japan, the situation was different:

> A man came to our seat and asked if I liked Japanese ciga-
> rettes. I said I did. He had Golden Bats. Then he asked if
> I'd like one. No, I wouldn't, thank you. Then would I
> exchange one for an American cigarette. No, I wouldn't,
> but I would give him a couple. Which I did. By now, three
> or four women were also crowded around. He then poked
> at me and said to Miss Matsumura, "How old is she?" After
> she interpreted, I answered, "Ninety-five." [When he heard
> that,] great exclamation of "*Ah, so desu ka!*" (Oh, is that so).

He then returned to his seat at the other end of the coach, apparently reporting the conversation all along the way. In his wake, we heard many more expressions of "*Ah, so desu ka*" as passengers rose in their seats to look at us. I sometimes wonder if a folk tale is still being told along the Sea of Japan about the old American woman on the train who was ninety-five but did not look a day over forty.

For centuries, a great gap had existed between the positions of ordinary Japanese people and Japanese officials. We Americans constantly tried to show that, in a democracy, the two can be brought closer together. When Miss Matsumura and I conducted meetings, we were considered important—and I more than she. So when possible, I insisted that she take the bigger chair of the two set for us on the platform. Once, when we were only observers at a social education conference in Ehime and had no part in the program, we had to work hard to avoid sitting in places obviously intended for us as "important people."

> [When we arrived,] we found the customary setup with places for important people. Ours, a table covered with a white cloth and a sign CIVIL AFFAIRS in Japanese, we ignored [and sat on a regular bench like everyone else]. Soon the white cloth labeled CIVIL AFFAIRS appeared in front of us. But we waved it away. I decided we had won. After lunch, the table minus the cover and sign was in front of the two seats we occupied in the morning. So we sat way in the back. We finally did win.

But did we? After all this time, I have to ask myself if those courteous people were aware that we were simply trying to be modest listeners and help them understand a democratic concept, or if they thought we were just being difficult.

Somewhat to my surprise, I found that my own place in the hierarchy was not constant. When we attended a conference not on our regular schedule, Miss Matsumura would examine the sign that customarily was posted outside the meeting place. "Only a -san today," she might announce when she read that Jonson-san would be the speaker. Or "Oh, today you are a -sama," a higher degree of honorific affixed to the last name. But she always spoke gleefully when she could say, "Today you are a -joshi," the term for a learned woman. Because I was apt to be a -san in the cities, a -sama in areas not quite so sophisticated, and a -joshi in the country, my importance to those in attendance was clear.

In January 1951, social education officials made plans for Mrs. Hayashi, Miss Matsumura, and me to hold meetings in Shikoku's four capital cities before my departure from Japan the following month. We requested that, in keeping with policies of the past three and a half years, no gifts should be presented and no meals offered, but we said that we would be pleased if the groups wished to serve tea and cakes for all as part of the program. I recalled the meetings in my journal: "My last meeting with women in Kagawa Prefecture. About twenty representing *gun* and cities. Almost all were older women. We had a good meeting, I think. I believe these women—and others like them—are sincerely trying to help the women of Japan." Ehime Prefecture also received a brief comment: "Met with women representatives at the CI&E library. [After my talk] they tried to force a present on me, but I refused. It was really quite unpleasant. But I was adamant so finally won." The women of Kochi Prefecture met at the prefectural library: "All told, twelve came. One from Muroto-misaki had started the day before. One from Matsubagawa—three o'clock this morning. Two from mountains north of Sukumo, the day before yesterday. They came 'over snowy mountains,' they said. Such desire to learn and better themselves. We had a pleasant, informal meeting."

The meeting in Tokushima Prefecture turned out to be unsettling and unpleasant, for the social education official (who should have been in charge) was weak and the federation president (whose organization should not even have existed) was dictatorial. After spending the morning on standards for an organization, there was time for recreation and some of the women danced. After lunch, the social education official was to present women governmental officials to the group, but the federation president plunked herself down in the middle.

> Then we got started again. I was at the question period when the federation president got up and started to make a speech. So I asked her to wait till I finished. In the meantime, along came a note from the chairman asking if the ladies could eat their cakes and fruit since it was an infor-

mal meeting. We ignored the note. Then I finished, and announced that I had [finished] to the social education woman in charge. The president then made a speech, and I was presented with a scroll of thanks. I started to pass it around so everyone could read it, when the president got her hands on it and read it aloud in an officious way. I was mad. We three civil education women had very fancy cakes, two bananas, and two tangerines. The rest had food not nearly as nice. Another thing that made me mad.

Some little time later, I asked the dancers if I could take their picture, saying we needed to go outside where there was enough light. They seemed pleased and "got in a circle, and there stood the president in the back. So I said she would have to get in the circle [as if she were dancing]. I guess I was just nasty by that time."

When I think about this meeting now, forty-five years after it took place, I find the account enlightening and, if viewed dispassionately, tragicomic. Two strong-willed women—the federation president and I—faced off for the final encounter, after never having come to an agreement about the prefectural federation. I was determined to be in charge of the meeting; she seemed just as determined to lead. I must have felt that everything that happened that day contradicted what I had tried to do in the past three years.

In fairness, one more comment must be made. The president of the prefectural federation, previously a wartime leader, must have felt her position threatened when the American women's affairs officer arrived on the island. She may have used this meeting to reassert her leadership to women of the prefecture precisely because I was leaving.

Assessing the results of my efforts on Shikoku is difficult. My task was formidable: to reach perhaps a million women directly or through their leaders to help them understand the national constitution and laws. This education was to take place in the space of a few years—a time period that barely amounted to seconds in the long history of Japan. For the women of Shikoku, the task was even more difficult: to grasp the meaning of democracy, equal rights, and government by the people in a country bound by ancient authoritarian and hierarchical concepts and ruled recently by militarists and ultranationalists.

Of course, more favorable changes may have taken place than we knew. The limited time we had to spend with women may have discouraged them from seeking us out for personal conversation. At the most, a working week was scheduled for each prefecture every other month, with three days in the capital city and two days in train travel. My efforts were thus spread very thin. In addition, women may have been hesitant to tell us about the smaller changes in organizational procedure, so we may have missed receiving word of those incremental steps.

However, many factors do indicate positive results: our invitations to meetings often resulted in audiences that numbered in the hundreds; presiding officers showed unexpected courage in asking men to leave meetings; leaders were eager to learn about parliamentary procedures, even if that meant assuming unaccustomed roles in skits; those attending meetings were willing to admit misunderstanding in such unfamiliar practices as making a motion and would request a second try; some *fujinkai* disassociated themselves from an established federation; most women seemed to understand the importance of having women speak out at meetings to express their own opinions; the women showed me great courtesy, attentiveness, and kindness; and they were generally willing to accept a member of the occupation as their mentor.

One remarkable instance in particular demonstrated how the people were beginning to internalize and act on democratic principles. For centuries the people had been told what to do by officials and they did it. Now the citizens of Hoshimachi were considering facing up to authority to correct a system they believed was corrupt. The confident Goliath—Mr. Okubata—was faced by an inexperienced, timid David—a combined effort of the local women's and youth groups. Mr. Okubata, a prominent citizen, was president of one of the two PTAs and chairman of the *minsei-iin* of Hoshimachi. The *minsei-iin,* provided for in the Livelihood Protection Law, were similar to social welfare organizations in America, but their scope exceeded that of comparable U.S. groups. The *minsei-iin* collected information on the living conditions and needs of people in their districts and then helped those identified as needy to get assistance—for example, financial help to support families or start businesses, medical treatment, including maternity care, and aid for funerals. Members served without pay; many were political appointees; and most, untrained in public welfare work, were unprepared to carry out the duties outlined by the law. The wide range of powers offered opportunities to unscrupulous members to do great harm.

In January 1950, the women and youth wanted to accuse Mr. Okubata of a range of offenses: unfair and biased practices as chairman of the *minsei-iin;* dishonesty related to the purchase of an organ for the town's nursery; dishonest handling of funds collected for the community chest; undue pressure upon the school principal against a woman in need; dishonest dealings regarding the PTA's purchase of material for the school; and undue influence upon the town officials in the purchase of land from his brother at a higher price than paid to other citizens who also sold land for public housing projects.

I made three suggestions for possible action. First, if the people did not want Mr. Okubata to be PTA president any longer, they should organize themselves to choose someone at the next election to replace him. Second, if Mr. Okubata had committed fraudulent acts as accused, they should make a report to the police or procurator. Third, the law provided for dismissal of a *minsei-iin* member by the Minister of Welfare upon advice of a prefectural governor. I told them the situation should be brought to the attention of the prefectural public welfare officials if any of the following reasons for discharge applied to Mr. Okubata: failure or inability to discharge his duties; neglect of his duties or violation of his obligations to his post; or conduct unbefitting a *minsei-iin* member.

One of the first steps taken by the *fujinkai* and *seinendan* was to collect evidence of Mr. Okubata's misconduct. They marshaled eight examples, complete with figures. In this effort, these women were consistent with a long history among Japanese women's groups of collecting and publishing evidence of malfeasance in public office.

Then, members of the *fujinkai* appealed for help to the local *minsei-iin*. After one of the committee recommended to Mr. Okubata that he resign, he did so—only to have his resignation refused by the mayor, who remarked that "the matter was a petty thing." When members of the *fujinkai* and *seinendan* asked the mayor why he refused the resignation, he assured them that Mr. Okubata would mend his ways. Events next took an unexpected turn when, in an election soon after, a new chairman replaced Mr. Okubata.

Next, the two organizations launched an attack upon Mr. Okubata for the role he played in the PTA. They prepared and distributed a statement about his alleged misconduct. Addressed "To all the people of Hoshimachi," it began, "We want to hear your thoughtful opinions about Taro Okubata, president of the PTA and *minsei-iin* member of this town." Following three examples of his alleged misconduct, the paper concluded that the

> head of the town knows everything written above. . . .
> Several people urged Mr. Okubata to reflect upon himself
> about his actions several times, but he relied on the support of the head of the town and the chairman of the town

assembly. . . . Are we the only people who entertain doubts about the head and chairman of the town assembly, because they are still supporting wholly Mr. Okubata, knowing everything about his past and present?

Following the distribution of this statement, representatives of the *fujinkai* and *seinendan* traveled to the prefectural capital and presented their case to public welfare officials. One of the women leaders, Mrs. Arita, wrote to me, "To our surprise who had guessed to have much trouble at the capital, the official was prompt to tell us that officials will go to the actual place to investigate on the next day. So we were pleased and told each other that we should have come to the capital earlier." When representatives of the prefectural welfare section visited Hoshimachi, they interviewed all persons concerned, leading Mrs. Arita to write again:

> We felt relieved believing that the case would be settled fairly. . . . But the mayor and the others spread various false reports about us. They said this disturbance was not made only by the *fujinkai* but that some people must have pulled the wires. . . . If people fight with those unconscientious men, they will be ruined. But we could not overlook misgovernment knowingly and roused ourselves to action against it. So I was much disappointed in the irresponsibility of government officials who ignored our sincerity but who tried to cover up this affair. . . . It takes time to democratize Japan. The way toward democracy lies in awakening our moral sense and [in electing] good representatives.

Soon the voices raised against Mr. Okubata extended beyond members of the organizations that had first raised the complaint. People were heard criticizing the town government, and newspapers began to disclose examples of mismanagement by town officials. And victory was achieved: Mr. Okubata finally resigned as a member of the *minsei-iin* and as president of the PTA. Mrs. Arita was pleased, writing to me, "I realized that heaven is sure to help people who are right. I suppose the town's people who kept sleeping for a long time will be awakened." She had been particularly encouraged by the accounts in the newspapers.

Perhaps her greatest gratification was expressed in another letter:

> Now people, who criticized the *fujinkai* at that time, saying that we, despite the fact that we are just women, were trying to interfere in the town's business, are beginning to cause the public opinion which means that the *fujinkai* did very well, so the *fujinkai* is in an important position.

In her last letter, she viewed the future with hope:

> We did not expect too much of the other people from the beginning regarding this case. . . . But I believe, in some time in the future, wave-rings in the water made by a stone of justice thrown by us will reach the banks.

6 · · ·

Pioneers

in Some

Way

Although most of my efforts during my years on Shikoku involved working with Japanese women through *fujinkai,* occasionally I had the opportunity to meet with women in other arenas—including *haha no kai* (mothers' clubs), women in labor unions, farm women, female factory workers, women staff members and elected officials, and women involved in organizing Girl Scout troops. Frequently, my experiences were similar to those I had with *fujinkai:* my goal was always to assist women in understanding their rights under the new government and to help them organize themselves into democratically run groups, independent of the government and of men, by which they could develop ways to improve their lives. And as with *fujinkai,* I often met similar obstacles: government officials and men who were determined to maintain control, and women who were generally shy and inexperienced.

One frustrating episode concerned *haha no kai.* A Ministry of Welfare document dated October 13, 1948, directed prefectural governors as follows:

> It is desired that *haha no kai* and child guidance groups be formed in your prefecture. . . . In order to conduct a

sound guidance of child life, first of all mothers must be informed correctly on how to guide the child's leisure hours, health, nutrition, way of living, and the like. *Haha no kai* will, therefore, be formed geographically (*Jihatsu* No. 693).

Prefectural documents then spread news of this directive to mayors, town and village headmen, principals of primary and secondary schools, and chiefs of child welfare institutions. Well! I can still recall my indignation, for such directives from above were directly opposed to the grassroots efforts we women's affairs officers had been trying to encourage. Mrs. Hayashi, my office assistant, discovered evidence of the consequences of this directive during a field trip she made by herself to a *fujinkai* in Tokushima Prefecture. She was surprised to find that a male official had also come to the meeting to establish by fiat a *haha no kai*. Her written report told what followed:

> A man from the village office told the members about the aim of the movement. He said, "Women should be mothers not only of their own but also of children in the whole country. From this point of view, you, women in a *fujinkai*, should agree to join the movement."
>
> "It sounds very good, I think," whispered someone.
>
> "Do you agree with it, everybody?" asked the chairman. . . .
>
> After a little discussion was held, the constitutions which he had made were distributed, in full speed, the president and other officers were appointed, and the organization set up, with the club getting confused with double constitutions and officers, while all the members were wandering in a dense fog.

Some time after my report on these incidents was forwarded to Eighth Army, Colonel Coughlin called me into his office. His first words to me were "General MacArthur doesn't like your reports." I knew that SCAP disliked criticism, but I wondered if he himself found time to read such reports. Nevertheless, I asked why. "They are too negative," he said; "are they?" I answered honestly, "They aren't. They are realistic—not negative." After we discussed the issue further, the colonel concluded that I should continue to write about situations as they existed if I had satisfactory confirmation. I heard nothing about a change in policy of the Ministry of Welfare and nothing more about negative reports.

Politics rather than government directives became the issue when, in 1949, I had meetings with two diametrically opposed groups of women from labor unions. In March, we met with sixty-five women from Kagawa unions: "They were young, alert, and interested. I may have trouble somewhere along the way, but so far most interesting." In contrast was a group in Ehime Prefecture that I met with in July:

> My, but it's hard to get a reaction from them! We acted like silly fools but could hardly get a glimmer. I finally experimented and asked direct questions of the women. One just simply refused to even lift her head to look at me. How in the world can we get around that!

What was the reason for such a difference? The answer was simple: both kinds of women belonged to unions.

As always, history was important. During the 1930s, as totalitarianism had vanquished any democratic tendencies, labor unions were suppressed. Then, after the war ended, when the occupation force encouraged the revival of labor movements, laws were revised so that unions could become powerful. Achieving this goal required careful monitoring, however, because there was also concern about the new power of communists in postwar Japan. In those first years of the Cold War, concerns arose partly because communists in Japan—who had been jailed under the totalitarian government—were freed by the occupation and, as part of the process of democratization, allowed to speak freely and run for office. The novelty of having communists operate openly certainly contributed to the concerns, although in fact their power was never extensive. Particular concern about communists surfaced in labor unions, especially as leaders with communist inclinations began to gain control of some unions. The women at the first meeting may have been from this energetic group, while many women—like those in the second group—were not vocal or active, even in unions where most of the members were women. This latter group of women tended to shun activity because many expected to work only until marriage, most were brought up to be shy and modest, and all believed that appearing assertive diminished their prospects for a good marriage. Separate women's sections in labor unions, therefore, were not unusual. In fact, before the war, separate women's sections had been a demand of feminist and leftist women, who saw them as a way to enhance women's power in male-dominated unions. In those I observed, however, members devoted time to such activities as the tea ceremony and flower arrangement rather than to workers' issues.

Farm women had their own special problems—and solutions. Agricultural cooperatives for farm workers were open to women, but because the husband was considered head of the family and thus spoke for all, few women ever joined. In fact, we never visited a farm cooperative meeting, for the numbers of women involved were too small. However, early in 1950, we learned that farm women in Kochi Prefecture had revived a very old form of a cooperative association—the *ko*. The first economic *ko* on record was organized in 3 B.C., when rice was stored from a good harvest to provide for the time of a poor crop. *Ko*—whether economic, religious, social, or a combina-

tion—differed from other organizations because they were usually formed voluntarily, were small with no dictatorial leadership
needed, were not controlled by the government, and did not try
to indoctrinate members or carry out reforms. However, *ko*
almost disappeared during the war years, when members were
forced to buy war bonds with money they might have contributed to the *ko* treasury. At that time, also, restrictions on
travel led to curtailment of *ko*-sponsored trips to famous shrines
or temples.

Then in 1950 some Shikoku farm women organized *ko* to
finance improvements in their kitchens. In one *gun* in Kochi Prefecture, twenty housewives banded together and paid a monthly
assessment of ¥300 (about eighty-three cents). The total ¥6,000
(about seventeen dollars) went each month to one member chosen by lot, until eventually all members had improved kitchens.
Other *ko* also included the bath and the well. It was rewarding to
see the old idea of the cooperative association revived to such
good advantage.

Of course, farm women did belong to *fujinkai* and often mentioned how hard it was to find time to attend meetings. In 1948,
the Kochi prefectural social education section compiled average
figures on how one hundred farm women said they spent their
days.

Activity	Hours
Farm work	8.20
Family	6.28
Friendly relations	.21
Recess	.80
Sleep	6.87
Doing nothing	.13
Culture and recreation	1.51
	24.00

Although "Doing nothing" and "Friendly relations" were perhaps the most intriguing, the more than eight hours daily spent on farm work in conjunction with more than six hours spent on the family demonstrated why women on farms had little time for organizations.

Like farm women, female factory workers suffered under a crushing system. At the first all-Shikoku conference of women officials in August 1948, Women's and Minors' Bureau (W&MB) chiefs had expressed concern about young women who were employed in factories and lived in dormitories where they worked. This system had a long history. During the first large-scale development of factories in Japan, in the Meiji period (1868–1912), young girls became workers. By custom and tradition going back to feudal times, daughters showed filial piety by allowing their fathers to sell their services under contracts with the factories. Leaving the farms in their late teens, the young women usually worked for a few years either to help with family finances or to earn money for a dowry. While working as little more than indentured servants, they lived in factory dormitories under strict supervision.

With some changes, this system was still in place during the occupation. A basic labor law passed by the Diet required better working conditions and ostensibly corrected one great abuse of the past: a farmer was no longer allowed to borrow money in advance in exchange for his daughter's work in a factory. But W&MB chiefs felt that the provisions of the new law were not being followed. I was told that a girl might be "bought" for factory work for ¥2,000 (a little more than five dollars).

When the chiefs asked me to visit some factories and dormitories, I agreed—asking them to decide where they wanted me to go. Although I knew very little about labor issues, I was pleased to try to help working women in any situation. In November 1948, we went with Miss Inage of Kagawa to three factories:

First a match factory that pays incredibly low wages and looks pretty horrible. . . . Then to two spinning factories, one in each of two towns. Particularly interested in the dormitories. They look fine — clean and airy. But Miss Inage says the bad part is the dorm supervisory system. I can well imagine there are abuses, but it will be hard to pin them down. "All is sweetness and light" on the surface. Supper at one place — sweet potatoes. The menu posted, however, looks fine.

These dorms are a selling point to get girls to come to work in the factories. One had a large recreation room with piano, a flower arrangement and tea ceremony room, a classroom where they could go to school while working.

A rayon mill was our destination when we visited Ehime:

First [we] visited the dormitory. Very large number of women here. Physical setup good. Six dormitories, each of which has a head. . . . Recreation room, beauty parlor, and bath. Average age of the young women is eighteen and a half Japanese count, seventeen and a half ours. Many looked like just children. . . . Saw kitchen and dining room. Bread, beans soaking (alive with bugs, swimming around), "spinach," white radishes, potatoes in evidence. Later, in conversation, I was told that in Kagawa Prefecture some factories black-market food. Here a committee from factory and workers checks food as it comes in to insure against black-marketing (so they say). . . . I made a great point that taking care of physical needs is not enough. I was asked by one of the officials to come back and speak to the dorm heads.

It is hard to assess the effect of our visits to these factories. One positive report came two months after our first visits to the Kagawa factories. Miss Inage reported that our visits to factory dormitories have resulted in activity by Japanese officials to check up on said dormitories. Meetings with heads—supervisors—or what have you— are being planned. Isn't it amazing what a casual visit can do? Also, isn't it regrettable that the visit of occupation personnel seems to make the Japanese jump when they [already] know something is wrong?

Even though improvements to the factory system during my time on Shikoku were slight, my hope was that such obvious interest in the young women and their well-being by a member of the occupation force would at least encourage Japanese officials to pay more attention to them.

After my first months in Takamatsu, plans and schedules fell into place, and the value of having Japanese women on the occupation teams became apparent. Officially, I was the only one on the island working in women's affairs. But unofficially and informally, each prefecture eventually also had a Japanese woman in that position. Although I was able to visit a prefecture only once a month at the most, the local woman was always available for consultations. At frequent all-Shikoku meetings in Takamatsu, the women and I shared our experiences with each other. One evening of these meetings was always devoted to social activities when I invited the women to the castle for refreshments—coffee or cold drinks (depending on the time of year) and candy, cookies, nuts, crackers, or whatever else the PX offered. On the first such evening, I stumbled over one of the many aspects of Japanese etiquette that always confused me. When I wanted to offer the women a second cup of coffee, I inquired, "Will you have some coffee?" The reply was always "Thank you." Since the answer was not "Yes, thank you" or "No, thank you," I never knew whether my guest really wanted the additional coffee I poured for her, just to be sure.

Although I enjoyed being with these women professionally, the little bits of information that came out in informal meetings delighted me even more. On one evening, "we were talking about my copy of the *Manyoshu*, a collection of Japanese poems [oldest of the early anthologies, of the seventh and eighth centuries]. Mrs. Inagaki said that, when they couldn't study foreign books, they studied these poems. She seemed very fond of them." At another social evening, the women discovered my boxed, two-volume set of *The Tale of Genji*, with color pictures on the front and back of the box. I could tell by their conversation in Japanese that they were distressed about something, and finally I asked what disturbed them. The pictures, they said, showed men and women wearing clothes and with their hair dressed typical of a period different from that of the novel. Although I wrote to the publisher about those points, the terse reply I received indicated my comments were not particularly welcome.

At one social evening in July 1949, three of the women, including Mrs. Hayashi, were in kimono. As we walked through the castle garden, I couldn't help thinking that they certainly fit into the picture beautifully. Several times I overheard them use the word *giri,* an often-used Japanese word that refers to debts that must be repaid with exactness to equal what was received. Later when I asked Mrs. Hayashi what the conversation was about, she reported that they wondered how they could ever repay *giri* for my kindness.

I recorded in my journal my last meeting with these women officials in January 1950: "They said they felt women had changed since I have been here. I wonder if that's really so. I believe they were sincere."

Still, on my final trips to prefectures in January 1951, I saw some discouraging signs. In Kochi, when I met with the secretariat people, I discovered that the woman official was expected to sweep the floors. She had another problem as well, for she knew that other officials falsified their travel accounts by putting down more days for travel than they were out. She wouldn't do that, so she had to spend her own money or work doubly hard trying to get in all her travel in the time she reports. I did what I could to help by raising these issues with region officials, but I'm not sure how much good I did.

Then, the following day in Tokushima, my spirits were lifted when Mrs. Hayashi, Miss Matsumura, and the social education official agreed that the status of women in social education was better because I had insisted that they were of equal status with men. In spite of this, my journal notes recorded my continuing concerns: "I wonder what will happen when I go. I can only hope some of the ideas will remain with the men. After all, we can't be 'big sticks' indefinitely."

In addition to the women's affairs officers of the military government, the Women's and Minors' Bureau had been established early in the occupation as a division of the Ministry of Labor. Although the bureau had an early history of ups and downs and the ministry announced at least three times that the bureau was to be abolished, in each instance the ministry backed off after vigorous protests by women's groups.

Gradually after the W&MB was set up, prefectural offices were opened with women as chiefs. Although they cooperated with government officials concerned with social education, public welfare, public health, and farm workers to help women as a group, a large portion of these chiefs' work was with working women, including members of labor unions. Because their objectives and mine were similar, I made regular visits to their offices on field trips and held all-Shikoku conferences to discuss common problems and solutions. At the first meeting, "in talking about principles of democracy, Miss Inage of Kagawa told of a labor union where 80 percent of the ballots cast were blank. She said the Japanese cannot make up their minds how to vote."

At a second conference about six months later, after discussing democratic procedures and policies all day, in the evening, we

> just talked. One thing we discussed was that Americans joke more than Japanese. Got on to family relations. I told them how my elder brother and I used to play tricks on my father [such as hooking up the alarm clock under the table to his dining room chair so the alarm would go off when he pulled out the chair to sit down]. They were quite upset. A Japanese father would have been angry, they said.

Looking back, I hope I made clear that no doubt some American men would have been angry at the tricks we played on my good-natured father.

During this time, I made several visits to the offices of women who were heads of their own governmental divisions. In these positions, they should have been given as good an office as a man in a comparable position. They were not, however—as always, it seemed because of the continuing inequality between men and women. On a visit to Miss Hara in Tokushima, we found her

> stuck in a room in the darkest corner, with a lot of Labor Standards Bureau inspectors. They were talking in loud voices as we came in but calmed down. The woman inspector was absent. Miss Hara should have an office to herself. On the first floor is a vacant room for serving tea. It would be fine for her! Maybe we can do something about it!

We must have done something, because on the next visit, I recorded in my journal that "Miss Hara was her usual talkative self. But I really think she is doing well. At least she has a decent office in which to work."

One final group of women whom I got to know slightly were elected officials. When meetings with female elected officials were scheduled in May 1948, I wondered what kind of women would attend. I was surprised to find them a very energetic, talkative group: "All [were] women in city or village assemblies. They were older. Believe most of them can hold their own with the men any time." Generally speaking, women who ran for office and were elected seemed quite different from the quiet, modest ladies I had met previously.

Earlier in my own career, I had been a volunteer Girl Scout leader for five years and then on the professional Girl Scout staff for six years. Knowing well the educational and socialization benefits of scouting for girls, I had wondered during my stay in Nagoya about setting up a troop there but was told the occupation force would have to investigate first. Later on Shikoku I discovered the reason for such caution when I learned that children's associations, like those for youth and adults, had been used for the purpose of military indoctrination during World War II.

But when Don Typer, youth affairs officer, CI&E, SCAP, visited Takamatsu in November 1947 and discovered my background, he approved adding Girl Scouts to our plans for Shikoku. The November 17, 1947, press release about my work announced, "Miss Johnson will help Japanese young women and girls form Girl Scout troops and will concentrate on training leaders and on finding sponsors." Two days later, prompted no doubt by that press release,

> a reporter came from the *Mainichi* [a newspaper] to ask if he could print a press release about me in an all-Japan release. That made us pause, since the Girl Scouts were involved. So Fred called Eighth Army. Decision was that the sentence in which "Miss J. hopes that in the future, etc. the Japanese Girl Scouts would be members of the World Federation" (news to us) was to be deleted.

The source of the reporter's interest turned out to be not the formation of Girl Scout troops but an American's expressing hope that the Japanese national organization would eventually become a member of the world body of Girl Scouts. Japan by that time was eager to become involved again in international efforts, and even a hint from an American in support of such a move would be encouraging. Unfortunately, I had not made such a statement. When it was deleted from the suggested news story, the reporter and his paper lost interest.

Publicity was one thing. But the really important challenge was establishing the troops and helping the Japanese come to an understanding of appropriate leadership and activities. Efforts to establish a Girl Scout organization at the national level were of interest to me, though unfortunately of little help. I attended with Mr. Typer an early meeting in Tokyo of twenty-two Japanese women working toward a national organization. The meeting was conducted by Mrs. Mishima, who headed the national committee and whose husband was the Boy Scout head in Japan. Also attending were two women from W&MB, some other women I understood were leaders, a woman formerly with the YWCA in Chiba Prefecture (near Tokyo), and a young woman who had taken a course in scouting during the year and a half she spent in the United States. I commented in my journal after the meeting, "it was an intelligent, interested group—but with no strong personality in it." Obviously, I had not yet learned that many women with leadership ability appeared quiet and unassuming.

Although I had only limited direct contact with the national organization after that meeting, we learned at one point that one of our Shikoku leaders had attended a Girl Scout leadership course in Tokyo. To my consternation, she had come away with two perplexing messages: first, no two patrols (small groups in a troop) in Japan could have the same name and Tokyo would assign the names; and second, that the city of Matsuyama could not have thirty-two in a troop. This incident caused me to comment in my journal on "such screwball ideas as the people in Tokyo have."

To move forward with the Girl Scouts on Shikoku, I needed to find a sponsoring body for each troop—an association like a women's group, a PTA, or a youth organization. I knew there were hundreds of such groups from which could come troop committees responsible for finding and assisting leaders and supporting troops. The point I kept stressing was that a firm foundation supported by sponsoring organizations was essential to distance the Girl Scouts from any hint of government control. After I wrote a pamphlet, "Girl Scouting on Shikoku," based on scouting programs in the United States, to use as a guide, we began traveling around the island to hold prefectural meetings for potential troop sponsors. To my delight, large groups began to appear. In Kagawa, for instance:

Had about 500 there. Most were young women—many teachers. . . . I ended by having them write down exactly what to do—even to writing me who all the people were, who were to lead troops, be on committees, etc.

A week later in Kochi:

The crowd filled the room to overflowing. . . . At the beginning, the man social education head appeared to hear about the Girl Scouts. I said that, since the prefectural women's affairs official was there representing the social education section, I felt she was capable of getting the material. I'd just been telling [the audience] not to let the government interfere. So why should I let a government official—and a man—come to the meeting? After the meeting, we went to call on the education chief . . . about letting women run women's affairs.

The story was different in Ehime: "Small group today. Most were girls from a normal school. Bit disappointing, but maybe we can get one troop anyway."

At the meeting in Tokushima, besides women we

had a bunch of normal school girls today. Also some men. But they did not return in the afternoon. . . . Mrs. Kushi [from the prefectural social education section] had some mimeographed song sheets we sang from after we finished. "Santa Lucia" and "My Old Kentucky Home" (for me, I presume). Then I asked for a Japanese song, and they sang "The Moon over the Deserted Castle."

The following month I began holding training sessions for leaders. Although the sessions generally went well, an unforeseen situation arose in Ehime Prefecture:

With great glee, I was informed that the teachers had picked twenty-four girls for the Girl Scout troop. The women had also met with the twenty-four. I told them very plainly that was very undemocratic and I would have none of it. If they wanted to continue that way, I was not interested in helping them. I said [the interpreter] and I would take a little walk for fifteen minutes and give them a chance to decide. . . . Well, they decided our way. So we continued the training class.

My opinion now is that I was not very democratic myself. But if I had not been decisive, we would have allowed a precedent to be set that Girl Scouting was open only to girls chosen by the teachers.

In May 1948 we attended the first troop meeting:

This is an auspicious day! The first troop in Takamatsu met. I was invited and took Mrs. Inagaki with me. About thirty little girls were there—all shapes and sizes. I could have hugged them. They seemed little but were fifth graders in the primary school. They giggled just like American youngsters. One thing I noticed was that they paid no attention to [me]—in this country a very unusual experience. They had three leaders, three troop commit-tee members, and the president of the sponsoring body. Very complete. The meeting went along very well. There were a few criticisms I could have made, but could do the same in the U.S.

They loved the sign and the handshake. Bless their old hearts! They took us to the jeep and all gave the sign and called "Sayonara."

June marked the first meetings of troops in Kochi. Twenty-three were at the first meeting, with three leaders:

Believe they're doing a good job. All sitting in a rectangle. On the side were many people: men teachers and princi-pal, president of the sponsoring body, and I presume troop committee. The president read a little speech. One of the girls moved over so she could sit down, too. Very nice. Said the laws. Played a game—much too difficult. Chil-dren had trouble catching on. One little girl even shed tears. Must speak about this. The program was written on the blackboard. All were wearing little trefoil [Girl Scout] badges.

The second troop met in a park. I was distressed that no lead-ers were present when we arrived and found the children there alone—a practice I had discouraged in the training.

One child had a whistle. When the leaders arrived, all lined up [at the whistle] in three lines, I presume by patrols. Much too formal and military. This was the sec-ond meeting of twenty-eight children and three leaders. Definite favoritism was shown the grandchild [of a promi-

nent *fujinkai* leader]. She was chosen [for special activities].
We must mention this favoritism thing.

The third troop of twenty-seven youngsters and three leaders
held its meeting

under a huge ginkgo tree on the playground. The leader
had a chart of the patrols and court of honor [patrol lead-
ers] setup. She explained very well, I think. It was their
third meeting. . . . The children acted scared. The leader
said they were shy. . . . The leaders were earnest but also
seemed scared.

Noichi-cho, near Kochi city, was our destination the next day,
when we found

sixteen Girl Scouts meeting in a kindergarten of one hundred children and three teachers run by the *fujinkai*. The
principal and two [school] inspectors came. We ignored
them. What business is it of theirs? Children are in patrols
with patrol leaders and officers. Had book for attendance
and dues. My, but they were good.

When the troop [meeting] was ready to begin, the
leader played on the organ. The children formed a line and
with a simple dance step made a circle. The kindergarten
influence was plain but how much better than the formal
beginning yesterday. The same procedure is followed when
going home.

Games, practice of promise and laws, dramatization of
laws. Then they embroidered their trefoil badges. . . . The
children have plans made until September. *Kamishibai* (paper
theater), entertainment for mothers, a nursery for children during the harvest are some of the plans.

On the following day, we drove to a troop in Susaki, twenty-
five miles and two hours by jeep from Kochi city. Along the way

we had a flat tire, and the driver had to take the tire to town to have it repaired. During the two-hour wait, we watched rice being planted in the little valley where we stopped and could see at close range the part women played in this farm work: "An ox was pulling a tool that was smoothing the ground. A man followed to finish the process by hand. Then women [standing in water] planted the rice shoots. A bamboo instrument [a long pole with teeth on one side] is used to line the shoots up. Shoots are placed along the teeth. The women worked remarkably fast."

Although I continued to meet with leaders on field trips, I could not make more regular visits to troops, as my time and effort were needed for other aspects of the civil education program. Beginning in March 1949, Mrs. Hayashi held some training sessions with troop committee members. As she started to make her preparations,

> she asked me what she should say. I told her to think it over. But she came back [a day or two later] with a blank paper. So we worked it out together. She said she had many ideas but could not organize them. I must not forget that most women have had no experience just as Mrs. Hayashi has not.

Although the Social Education Law of May 22, 1949, specifically forbade prefectural and local government interference with organizations, keeping the Girl Scouts independent remained a constant struggle for me. In December 1949, for example, the social education official in Tokushima told me "that Social Education is sponsoring Boy Scout leadership training and wants to do the same for the Girl Scouts. No go, I said." That Tokushima officials still did not understand the meaning of the new law became apparent again when, in February 1950, I was invited to visit a troop sponsored by a church and learned that "the Social Education people brought questionnaires to all troops asking all kinds of questions. It is impossible to make them understand that the Boy Scouts and Girl Scouts are private organizations. The minister said, 'They don't have enough to do.' How true."

Another troublesome question was the part teachers tried to play in the Girl Scout program. In the past and during the early years of the occupation, education had been in the hands of the Ministry of Education and, by extension, in those of teachers under its orders. At meetings related to the Girl Scout program, a goodly number of teachers were always present. My note after a July 1949 meeting in Kagawa could be widely applied: "This old business of everything the children do being the teachers' business certainly is true."

As both girls and boys became involved in their scouting programs, problems arose about men interested in Girl Scouting. As early as December 1947 in Takamatsu, "I had a Boy Scout man call. He has been asked to start a Girl Scout troop by the girls. Told him to tend to his boys and let the girls tend to their business. When he has some interested women, then I'd help him." Two years later, again in Takamatsu, "The Boy Scout office invited Girl Scout leaders to a meeting. We got the meeting into our office, and I ran it. Believe these Girl Scout leaders will let us help them instead of turning to the Boy Scouts. Think we've spiked the guns of the aggressive Boy Scout man."

Encouraging national news, however, came in May 1950, when Mrs. Kimi Hara, first national director of the Girl Scouts, told me that an entirely new set of officers had been elected at the national convention. The first woman to preside had announced that only those candidates nominated by committee could be voted upon. When Mrs. Hara bravely protested, the group finally agreed to allow nominations from the floor. She said there was trouble in doing all this, and it was very difficult because the women were unaccustomed to such procedures. But finally officers and board were elected. I was thrilled to hear of this and noted in my journal that night: "I think this is really a remarkable procedure. Here are surely the beginnings of the idea of democracy. That the old crowd was thrown out legally and in good order is certainly a good sign. Maybe we are making some progress after all."

Overall, I was pleased with the progress we made in establishing Girl Scouts on Shikoku. Just before I left the island, representatives of the troops and their leaders in Tokushima met with me to say thank you and presented me with three dolls— one made by the girls, the others by the minister's wife of the church troop. This gift created a serious dilemma for me, as I stood listening to the little speech of thanks. The leaders knew I did not accept gifts because I could never repay the givers. But would ten-year-olds understand? My usual stubbornness regarding gifts melted at the prospect of seeing disappointment on their faces. Fortunately, I thought of a solution in time and announced that I would accept the dolls on the condition that I could give them to Girl Scouts in the United States. And I did.

All of the working women I met were pioneers in some way. They were disadvantaged by the inferior education provided girls and women; constrained by social pressures to exhibit only ladylike and modest behavior; and ill-equipped or lacking in administrative or business training and experience. Elite women were circumscribed by thousands of years of tradition that discouraged women from working outside the home; if they did work, they were poorly paid and often subject to family disapproval. Like elite women, those women who labored on farms and in shops and factories had no rights; nevertheless, they had to work, usually for long hours and little or no pay. In spite of the difficulties, all these women persevered and made great strides for themselves and their country during this period, while also retaining the admirable qualities of Japanese women. For them, I still feel great respect.

7 · · ·

Encounters

Beyond the

Office

I n August 1945 in San Francisco, when I was a WAC with the
Fourth Air Force, I heard the emperor's historic broadcast
announcing the surrender of Japan. The reception on my radio
was full of static, and sounds often faded away as I lay in bed late
that night listening to the thin, high-pitched voice of the emperor
telling his people the war was lost. Little more than a year later,
I was in Nagoya when the emperor visited in October 1946. On
my way to the hotel for lunch, I was held up at a street crossing
by a cavalcade of cars, one of which held the emperor. As I
recorded the occasion in my journal:

> Great crowds [were] gathered near the Chiyoda Hotel, but
> I missed him. I understand the people bowed and cheered
> *"Banzai"*(Long life to the emperor). When I [remarked] to
> Mrs. Nakano that it wasn't a very nice day because it was
> raining, she said this had been a very nice day because she
> had seen the emperor. She had tears in her eyes.

Between those two dates, the new constitution for Japan was
first proclaimed to the people. (It was then adopted in May
1947.) According to Article 1, "The emperor shall be the sym-

bol of the state and of the unity of the people, deriving his position from the will of the people with whom resides sovereign power." With the emperor's position thus greatly changed, he became a secular symbol of Japan and people could for the first time look directly at him, although he was still never referred to by his name but always as "the present emperor." On the other hand, many Japanese—especially older citizens—continued to hold him in great respect and reverence. In a discussion once about *chu,* or obligation to the emperor, Mrs. Hayashi told me that *chu* was changing: "Ten years ago, when [the emperor] came down here, old people knelt and bowed. Some old ladies threw coins like they do at a shrine. He was that to them." Since his change in status also meant a change in official duties, he began to appear throughout Japan; but because he was shy, he found difficult the small talk so necessary for public figures. Some Americans nicknamed him "Mr. *Ah, so desu ka*" (Mr. Oh, is that so?) from his habit of using that common expression in conversation instead of more fitting remarks.

To many Americans with the occupation, the emperor was a distant figure of little interest; some had only the haziest—often mistaken—ideas about him and his family. On a conducted tour on a weekend trip to Kyoto in January 1947, I joined other occupation members for a visit to the emperor's summer villa. The estate was famous for the Katsura gardens and contained perhaps half a dozen houses. A young American wife "commented to me on how many rooms there were. I said I supposed an emperor had quite a retinue. She said, 'Oh, yes, he has lots of wives, doesn't he?' I made no comment. 'He does, doesn't he?' 'No, I believe he has one.'"

When we learned in February 1950 that the emperor was to visit Shikoku the following month, the Americans were told to leave all arrangements to the Japanese and not to interfere with or enter into ceremonies or schedules. I did hear some gossip about local elected officials using the visit for their own political purposes. Apparently, each governor had been allowed to arrange the emperor's itinerary for his prefecture, but one had chosen locations where he needed support for the next election. And because the same governor had supposedly been treated rudely by the maids in the best hotel in one city, he decided that the emperor would instead stay in a factory dormitory in a nearby town.

All around us we saw preparations for the emperor's visit. In Ehime, camouflage left over from the war was finally removed from the exterior of the prefectural building. In Takamatsu, I saw evidence of tidying up when I rode my bicycle to Ritsuriin Park. Famous nationally for its beauty, the park was laid out in the latter part of the sixteenth century by the first feudal lord of the area, the same man who built the original Tamamo Castle. Now, I recorded in my journal the preparations in the park for the emperor's visit: "People busy cleaning up a stream. Stones being removed and muck cleared out. I presume the stones will be washed and replaced." In fact, as a consequence of the general refurbishing throughout the island, some began to call the emperor *hoki,* or broom.

The directive that Americans were not to participate in events of the emperor's visit was broken three days before his arrival: "It seems the emperor likes oatmeal. . . . But there is none in Kagawa Prefecture. The cook called one of the interpreters to see if the Americans had any. So Martha and Doug Campbell [our legal officer] came through with half a box." And I had a hand in bending the rule if not breaking it when Mr. Masao Wada, a scholar on our staff, was chosen to spend fifteen minutes with the emperor telling him the history of Kagawa and describing the twelve national treasures assembled in Ritsuriin Park's Art Hall for his viewing.

Because the civil education chief was on a field trip at the time, Mr. Wada asked me if he could be excused for this meeting. Two considerations arose in my mind: first, Mr. Wada, as a

Japanese staff member with the occupation force, technically should not participate in this activity; and second, he should get permission from the regional commanding officer if an exception were to be made. I knew that I should go to this officer for approval, but I also knew that he had previously shown little sympathy for the Japanese and regularly spoke of them as "those monkeys"—so I feared that his answer would be no. Well, I did what any right-thinking person should do: I didn't ask him. Instead, I gave *my* permission for Mr. Wada to meet the emperor.

On March 13, 1950, "great excitement. The emperor arrived in Takamatsu. Since no one from civil education was supposed to go to see him, we watched from the window. We knew from hats and flags being waved when he passed the corner a block away." Mr. Wada returned to the office after his fifteen minutes with the emperor and carefully hung up the long-tailed coat of his formal dress. He was still clearly moved by the experience, telling us the emperor "was only—this far away. He is a very fine gentleman." I said, "Did he ask any questions?" "One," Mr. Wada responded. "He asked if those treasures were always left here." Apparently the emperor was still having trouble knowing what to say and how to say it.

My indirect encounter with the emperor was one of many experiences I had during my time on Shikoku that were not related to my official duties. These episodes provided a broader portrait of Japan during the occupation period and the many types of interactions that occurred each day between individual Japanese citizens and members of the occupation force. These interactions were virtually always interesting and generally pleasant for me, so I was surprised, after returning to the States, when a friend asked if I'd ever been afraid in Japan. My first reaction to her question was "Why should I have been?" Generally, I felt safe walking the streets of cities alone, riding trains on which I was the only non-Japanese passenger, and traveling by jeep in remote areas where an American had never been before. But on two occasions, although I was not genuinely afraid, I did feel concern about how to extricate myself from troublesome situations.

While stationed temporarily in Tokushima, I decided to visit the dentist at the army hospital in Kobe, my last checkup having been more than a year earlier. Since Kobe is on the main island of Honshu, traveling there meant taking a ferry. On a small, private, off-limits ferry, the trip on the Inland Sea took five hours. On the authorized government ferry from Takamatsu, the trip took thirteen hours and also required train travel. Consequently, the team had given official orders to its members to ride on the off-limits ferry, even though safe passage could not be ensured because the waters there had not been swept for mines as thoroughly as had those on the official route.

On this trip, I had a pleasant, uneventful ride on the small ferry from Komatsushima along with the team doctor, who also was visiting the clinic. My teeth, it turned out, needed no attention except cleaning. When the dentist finished, he said, "Now, where is your husband?" Sometimes even Americans did not think that a woman and man could be traveling together as professional colleagues!

The following morning, I was to return alone to Tokushima:

Since there is some question in the minds of the Japanese about our using the ferries, we started at eight o'clock to get it all straightened out. The captain rode down in the jeep with me. At nine-thirty, we were assured that all was well, I was ushered into an inner office, the captain left, and then I was told that I could not go on the ferry.

I had only thirty minutes to talk myself onto the ferry—which I hadn't much hope of accomplishing, frankly. I told the official to call Kobe Base Information desk. He called someone, but I don't know where. Finally he asked me if I would be punished if I were doing wrong. When I assured him I would, he seemed to think it was OK, and I got my ticket.

Then he asked for my orders. I had only one copy so wouldn't give that up. All in all, it was rather unpleasant. When I asked for someone to take me to the ferry, he was uncooperative but finally got me a redcap. After depositing me and luggage in the first-class lounge, the porter asked me for money. That was the wrong thing—and I did not fork over. The captain had said we don't tip, and I was darned if I'd be put upon just because I was a lone female.

Now as I think back on this experience, I believe that I can understand better why such unpleasantness—rare as it was— occurred. The Japanese official had authority on his side, of course, to refuse passage on a ferry unauthorized by SCAP even though I had orders from the team officials. But why did he agree that I could sail when the captain was with me and then decide later that I could not? Was his action based on my being a woman? Perhaps I was supposed to give in meekly when he told me I could not sail? Did he then relent when responsibility was transferred from him to me after being assured that I would be punished if trouble resulted? Why did he decline to get a redcap quickly? Could that have been because, if he did, he was showing tacit approval for presumably unauthorized passage? And, finally, I know now that I should have tipped the redcap. Since this was not a Japanese National Railway ferry, he would not have been employed by the government as were redcaps on authorized allied trains and ferries, and he thus had to depend on tips from passengers for part of his income. In spite of my better understanding of the incident in retrospect, I will always remember how helpless I felt when told I could not ride on that ferry. This was my first experience alone when no Japanese acquaintance was present who could explain my position in a country where as, first, a civilian, and second, a woman, I had little status.

In February 1948, Stella Hoshimiya (my housemate in the castle) and I managed to acquire bicycles, thereby gaining a means of pleasure, exercise, and transport all in one. When we first began to ride about the city, I wondered why Stella insisted that I take the lead. Sometime later, she confessed that she liked to ride behind me to hear what the Japanese said about "the old lady on the bicycle" (I was then almost thirty-eight).

One of our favorite rides was to Ritsuriin Park. On Easter 1948, when the cherry blossoms were in bloom, our destination was the shop of a photographer in the park. As we rode up, I noticed a dozen or so young people on the grass just across from the shop. Bottles were in evidence, and at least one girl in kimono was smoking. I noticed a large basket and thought it looked quite like a picnic at home. Inside the shop, after Stella and I gave the photographer our film to be developed, we looked around a bit.

> I was pricing some little notebooks when a commotion began behind us. A young man dressed in kimono, all loose and partly off, began talking in loud tones to the young clerk waiting on us. I believe a couple of other young men were with him.
>
> Stella and I backed away and walked over to the left of the shop. Suddenly [the young man] pushed the glass case backwards, where it crashed to the floor. We handed back the booklets we had in our hands and "beat it."
>
> As we rode off toward the park entrance, Stella said it was because of us that it happened. The man said something to the shopkeeper about his "catering to occupation personnel," as Stella put it. Then I did feel bad. We consulted as we rode along. I thought we'd better inform the OD [the military government's officer of the day], although the matter was for the Japanese police.

After some time trying to find a place where we could call, we met a policeman on the street. We told him our story, and he went back to the shop with us.

> The case was back in place, the glass all pushed together in a dustpan. We told [the shopkeeper] we had brought a policeman. Soon he appeared with a young man—not the one who pushed over the case. They talked to the shop-keeper, the policeman took some notes. Finally all bowed and turned to go. Another policeman had appeared by now.
>
> I asked if the police had the name of the culprit. We were told the damage would be taken care of. The young man "*sumimasen*'d us." He looked scared. [*Sumimasen* can mean "I am sorry" or "I apologize" as well as "thank you for the trouble you went through."]

I felt a twinge of regret every time we visited the photographer's shop after that and I saw the case still standing without glass—a commodity so expensive and hard to obtain that the owner could not replace it. And I resented very much that the offender, hav-ing given a fictitious name and incorrect address to the police, had not been apprehended and forced to pay for repairs. I have always felt that this unpleasantness was caused by a drunken young man and that it was not a deliberate attack against mem-bers of the occupation force. But sometimes I wondered if the situation would have been different if we had been men or if we had been wearing military uniforms.

In the autumn of 1950, when the occupation was closing down and my departure seemed certain for early 1951, I began to form a plan to visit Shikoku's southern crescent to talk to people who lived far from the major population centers. No railroads tra-versed the half-moon southern coast of the island. On the east, the rail line ended at Hiwasa in Tokushima; on the west, at Uwajima, Ehime Prefecture. Travel was possible only by jeep from Hiwasa south and around Cape Muroto, which juts into the Pacific Ocean, and then north to Kochi city, or from Uwajima south and around Cape Ashizuri and north to Kochi city. Although the large-scale map from the army map service showed the roads around the eastern coast from Hiwasa to Kochi as national highways, those from Uwajima to Kochi around the western coast were prefectural roads. National roads were said to be "all-weather" and prefectural "usually metalled" (surfaced with broken stones). Their widths were the same: "over 4 m. wide," or about thirteen feet. When I thought about the many Japanese in those remote regions who were seldom if ever visited by civil education officials—and reflected that I might learn something about what the occupation had, or had not, accomplished in rural areas by traveling there—any concerns about creature comforts faded. And, to be honest, I wanted to visit those distant areas as well because of their reported scenic beauty.

I got approval for two trips—one beginning down the east coast, the other down the west—and my interpreter, Miss Matsumura, and I made our plans. Since my primary interest was still with women, we first requested meetings with them. Also included on the schedule were consultations with town and village officials about adult education, PTAs, and citizens' public halls (CPHs), which an American would probably call community centers. Legally provided for in the Social Education Law, the halls in some areas were housed in separate buildings; in others, a school or the town or village office was the site.

Our first trip began on October 6. When we arrived in Kuwano, our first stop, we discovered there was no CPH building:

In fact, everything is still on paper, since this is a very new CPH. Mr. Amano, the prefectural CPH official, had said this was a "baby CPH." So I made such a remark to them.

The headman who was also the CPH manager said I had given the baby mother's milk. Well, that's a new one for an *oludo missu*.

We reached "Mugi, our destination for the night, in the middle of the afternoon. Met with town officials. I was quite impressed with their being 'on the ball.' Lower-secondary school principal, who speaks English quite well, is CPH manager. The inn gave us two adjoining rooms on the top floor." I don't know how the inns were reimbursed since expenses for housing members of the occupation force were borne by the Japanese government, not by the military government. No doubt the inn was not crowded in Mugi, because I asked Miss Matsumura to inquire if I might have more than one quilt to sleep on. After considerable conversation, the maid with much giggling "fixed me a 'throne' of eight quilts and a cover. I was very comfortable as the bed was not even hard. Miss Matsumura did not recommend the bath so I washed in cold water. The latrine was down a horrible little flight of stairs. Quite cool here."

At the meeting next morning with the CPH advisory committee,

> One man introduced himself as a "good-natured man." He had gaps in his teeth and was not very neat. In the middle of the meeting, he realized he didn't have on his necktie. So he pulled it out and put it on. Everyone laughed, including him.
>
> [The CPH has] four branches, one on a little island visible from [where we are]. There was concern expressed about the difficulty of getting the fishermen to meetings. One committee member is a fisherman. Often he cannot attend because he is fishing. On Teba Island [the one visible], there are meetings on "full-moon nights." The women all come, but the men cannot as they are fishing. But the women go home and tell the men, so much good comes of the meetings.

When after lunch we stopped for a time by the water, a crowd gathered. Miss Matsumura reported that "one woman said I was 'so luxurious.' I was wearing stockings for one thing. I was dressed in a dress I've worn for four summers, old snagged nylons, loafers patched and repaired and three years old, and my WAC sweater that is eight years old. Luxury!"

At our afternoon meeting, we met with representatives from the PTA and the *fujinkai*:

> Eleven women (all old but one) and all in kimono sat on one side. The one woman on the other side represented the PTA. As we came in, a man with a scraggly beard, teeth missing, and not too well dressed said, "Good evening." And this at one o'clock. So I answered, "Good evening." He was a character, but everyone seemed to respect him. He was a doctor. We met another doctor in the morning—precise, neat. Quite a contrast.
>
> Questions were very interesting. Do you sign your name to a ballot and why not? If a tie in America, do you always draw lots? If the president chooses other officers and all the people agree, is that OK? (Our bearded friend said, "I didn't do that!") What is freedom? He wanted to ask an American that, since Americans know about freedom. . . . There are about 1,500 women in the *fujinkai*. So I got in a whack about interest groups. . . .
>
> I liked the Mugi people. The mayor took us to see a new lower-secondary school and then to the port. The Nankai earthquake of 1946 did much damage to Mugi. The seawall sank. This is quite a little port. Millions of children followed us there. The little boys all kept wondering if I had on stockings. They knew Miss Matsumura did [hers were heavy], but they couldn't decide about me. So we stopped, and I showed them I had on stockings.
>
> When we got back to the inn, we found a letter from

the lone young woman who had been at the meeting. She had just gotten up her courage to say something when we stopped. I guess we still don't know what trouble it is for women to speak out.

After supper, we took a little walk. There isn't much to this town—at least where we were. We stopped in a little shop. The woman owner was talking to a woman [apparently a vendor, who had] a tin can tied up on her back. While we were looking around, she began to count out candy drops from the tin. She said we must wonder about her working so late. She was "ashamed" to be doing so, but she was a widow with three children.

Because the next day was Sunday with no meetings scheduled, after a leisurely breakfast we left about ten o'clock for the three-hour drive to Muroto, crossing the boundary into Kochi Prefecture in about an hour:

Beautiful ride. Much of the time we drove right along the ocean. The mountains rise sheer from the sea, with a narrow little road cut out. Once in a while there is a wide space where a village nestles. Some houses have stone walls along [the road] here. In other places, the high stone walls surround the houses, cutting out wind and sea—also light and air, I'm sure.

The coast is very different here and much more forbidding than that of the Inland Sea. No islands, just the expanse of the Pacific. Big boulders and black sand. I had heart failure a few times when we met a bus or truck on a curve. But nothing happened, fortunately. Our driver went a little too fast to suit me. I'm glad it wasn't wet.

Near our destination, after we drove around Point Muroto, we began to go north on the east side of Tosa Bay toward Kochi city. When we arrived, our inn was spacious, and our rooms overlooked the ocean. We were the only guests at this beautiful spot, so we had the second floor to ourselves. After lunch, we walked around a bit on the beach. The waves broke in lovely foam over huge boulders that had risen up out of the ocean at the time of the Nankai earthquake. What a sensation that must have been for the people to wake up in the morning to find those rocks there. At bedtime, I "decided a cold wash in a little basin was better than the communal tub. Warm here. Had a 'quilt throne' again."

We contacted the town office by telephone early on Monday and changed our schedule at the request of Muroto officials, since the Hachiman Shrine festival (a Shinto celebration) was to take place on the next two days. We started out at nine-thirty for our ten o'clock appointment, and in ten minutes, we were at the town office:

> Miss Matsumura and I got out, told Manabe-san [our driver] we would leave about three-thirty, and went in. No one knew anything about our coming. Inquiry disclosed we were at Muroto-misaki, not Muroto-cho. With no driver in sight, we got a bus — just in time — and climbed aboard. We told the officials to send the jeep after us. Before long, the jeep was chasing us. Manabe-san had gone to buy . . . *hanagami* (tissue) for me. Having not found any, he had gone back to the office, been told our plight, and started after us.

After he caught up with us, we disembarked from the bus and climbed into the jeep — giving the bus passengers a story to remember.

> We arrived on the nose — ten o'clock. We were told they knew we were very prompt and wondered where we were. Then just at ten, we arrived. Shoes were removed at this town office before entering.

The officials gathered were a queer mixture. Two young women—one welfare and sanitation problems and one construction and education. I think [their presence] was "a front" for me, as when I asked questions, they knew nothing. Also had a chief of sanitary problems and welfare. The headman said not much had been done in social education. He was "ashamed" to admit it. Then he muttered about typhoons. Blame everything on the weather, brother! I can believe that not much has been done. No CPH, no advisory committee, no *fujinkai*, no nothing. There is a widows' organization because "they need to encourage each other." The mayor said too many committees had been formed after the war. He was confused by it all. A rather pitiful place really. . . . I definitely felt the difference between Mugi and Muroto—both about 10,000 population. One is active, one is the opposite.

At the close of the meetings we returned to the inn. Before retiring, I asked for a large mosquito net that filled the room, hanging from the four corners: "Too many pests last night. Then I killed a huge roach playing around my throne. Later in the dark, I heard a 'plop' on the *tatami*. It was a spider 'surrounding' the roach. The wind came up, and it is raining."

When we left our inn the next day in a hard rain, we discovered that the back window of the jeep had no covering and the roof leaked like a sieve. Although no one could keep dry under those conditions, I was then especially glad that some time earlier, I had obtained raincoats by mail for Miss Matsumura and Mrs. Hayashi. When we arrived in Tano-cho, we asked several people where the CPH was, but no one knew. After searching out the town office, we learned that we were expected there since no CPH existed. Present at the meeting were the vice mayor, a bored assemblyman, the alert young man who was the CPH manager, four town committeemen, and several people standing along the walls—but no women.

Questions were varied. What kinds of CPH activities are in the U.S.? Do you have *seinendan* in the U.S.? Are PTA programs different there from in Japan? What methods are used to help children and young people understand the situation in foreign countries? Americans and communism are fighting. How can teachers give guidance to children? Nine billion yen [come] from PTAs to schools. There may not be enough money. . . . Will Johnson-san please write to the Ministry of Education to be sure there is enough money? . . .

More heart failures till we got to Aki. The ride would have been beautiful on a nice day, as we skirted the bay almost all the way. We arrived in Aki soaked, muddy, and chilled. It was good to be there. Paved streets, lights, and tall [two- and three-story] buildings seemed a change from the country where we had been.

The inn wasn't much. But we had an upstairs wing of eight-mat and six-mat rooms, with latrine. A forestry conference of all-Shikoku was meeting there. . . . When we went to wash, [we met] men wandering around in their underwear to and from the bath. . . . Rice wine seemed to be flowing freely. I didn't even wash that night but decided cold cream would do. Only three quilts tonight.

[On the following morning] when Miss Matsumura called the town office at nine o'clock, they knew nothing of us. Mayor and vice mayor were in Tokyo. The vice mayor had gotten the letter about us, made inn reservations, and nothing more. But we went at ten o'clock to see what we could find.

We were squired throughout the day by the official responsible for accounts. Perhaps he was the senior official. We met an assortment of people — registration-of-family official, document official (pretty girl), welfare people, two assemblymen. . . . A CPH is about to begin operations. One assemblyman seemed like an energetic,

intelligent soul. No adult education since the summer of
1949. . . . Aki sometimes has meetings where famous pro-
fessors from universities speak. What does that mean to
the farmer and fisherman? But there is hope in the energetic assemblyman.

After lunch, saw twenty-four PTA and women's organization people. The women belong to the . . . widows'
club, plus a fancy sounding group of "leading women." The
president [of that group] has probably been that for fifty
years. . . .

We stopped at three o'clock. By three-thirty we were
on our way to Kochi—in the rain. Arrived at the BOQ at
five. I certainly was glad to anticipate a good meal, a bed,
and a bath.

In nine days, we had had twenty-four conferences: "We saw
many people, talked about many things, and got in a good many
licks. I learned many things firsthand that I had suspected before.
The drives were a bit harrowing, but the scenery was beautiful.
All in all, a satisfactory and enjoyable trip."

A month after our return from the trip to the eastern horn, we
began the second long trip—this one around the western side of
the crescent—with the first leg on The Eagle. After a day in
Matsuyama, we went to Uwajima for meetings with social education people in the morning and, in the afternoon, the PTA:

Two interesting things happened. One was about the
fujinkai city federation composed of seven units. The units
meet together and vote about some joint projects. One
unit may not want to do it, but *tasu* (a large majority)
voted for it. The speaker felt sorry for the minority.

The other comment was about [Shinto] shrine festivals.
There are ten shrines and formerly each had its own festival day. The women work hard to prepare for the festival.

Even strange men come and drink rice wine at their homes. So the women wanted all the festivals on one day. A survey was made and 89 percent (of whom I'm not sure) agreed. But a few men were very vocal, so they could not have all the festivals on one day but on two or three days. So [they asked] did democracy really work?

At our first stop in Iwamatsu, we met with town officials and the CPH advisory committee. The mayor, newly elected, was "all done up in a black, formal coat." Education was in the hands of a young man who seemed pretty good. Later we moved over to the CPH, where there was a stove, for meetings with women and PTA representatives. There we learned that

> the *fujinkai* is not active. The former president was [at the meeting]. She had been president for twenty years, but refused [to serve] again in March 1950. There are 970 members. The PTA president said if she didn't take office, no one else would, as no one else was capable. Later one of the women said a few women (100) may form an interest group. Of course, I heartily concurred.

After lunch, we left for Misho on a beautiful drive along the broad channel stretching toward the horizon and Kyushu Island to the west:

> We noticed peculiar terracing. The terraces are all supported by stones. This is distinctive in this part of the country. Also noticed thousands of slices of sweet potatoes drying in the sun. All along the way, we saw people harvesting sweet potatoes [in Japan they are more grayish than orange].
>
> We blew into Misho—literally—to find about a dozen people gathered, including two *gun* officials. The mayor is a dentist, who is quite a talker. The CPH is on paper and really hasn't started yet. We had a very friendly, informal sort of talk.

Our stop for the night was an inn in Johen, Ehime Prefecture. A caller in the evening, a dentist, wanted "to tell us about the bosses who rule Johen. His story seemed biased in at least one respect. But he wanted civil affairs to do something [about the bosses] before the peace treaty was signed and we all went home. Of course, I told him it was up to the Japanese people to settle the problem themselves." When we met the mayor of Johen the following morning, "I wasn't surprised after our conversation of the night before with the dentist [to find him] a meek and mild headman. The official in charge of social education wasn't even there—he was gathering sweet potatoes. . . . In fact, I was not much impressed with anything about Johen."

After we ate lunch there, we drove to our overnight stop at Sukumo in Kochi, seeing much harvesting of sweet potatoes en route. "The sun was out, and it was much warmer. We followed a river part of the time, at a slower clip [after we so requested the driver]." Although we went through some hair-raising experiences on this trip, I felt more confident with his driving. One time, when I told him how pleased I was that he was so careful, he replied that he was responsible for two lives. I corrected quickly with "three lives. You must count yours, too."

In Sukumo, "I wasn't much impressed with the mayor. The official in charge of education is a woman—obsequious, fawning, and too darn polite. She was so busy rushing around about us and telephoning that she didn't talk to us until we asked about some things the mayor didn't know. No CPH, no social education advisory committee, no adult education." In retrospect, I suspect the woman was worried about our visit, concerned because no reports could be made about so many aspects of social education, and unsure of just how to treat us. Thus, as a Japanese woman, she was very polite—too polite, it seemed to me—so she appeared "obsequious" and "fawning."

We went upstairs to meet PTA and *fujinkai* representatives. There were about fifteen women, four men, and five high school girls. Of course, I presumed the men represented the PTA. But to my amazement, the women put up their hands when asked [who was from the PTA]. So I facetiously said, "I suppose the men represent the *fujinkai*." And, by golly, they did. The women couldn't come, so the school principals came to represent them. That sounds a bit fishy but is how it was explained. . . . [T]o all appearances the PTAs are good. They seemed to understand what I was talking about in regard to a good organization.

The trip the following day between Sukumo and Shimizu began at half-past nine and ended at two, although the distance as the crow flies was only some twenty miles. We had planned to take the road south and then east along the seashore via Misaki, but a bridge was under repair, so we took an inland route first east and then south: "We drove over a little, narrow road where we met only half a dozen vehicles. The road went through wild, wooded country until we got to the coast. Drove along a river— Nakasujigawa—for much of the inland trip. Beautiful drive, though the roads weren't very good."

Shimizu was at the base of the rounded thumb that was Cape Ashizuri. After we arrived at the inn and had a little rest, we

went for a walk. Talk about the Pied Piper! All down the street ahead and behind us were all the people staring out at us. We were told at the inn that, as far as they knew, [I was] the only American [woman] to visit Shimizu.

On Saturday as we started off for a meeting at ten o'clock with town officials, it began to rain, and we drove to the office in a downpour:

The vice mayor, education officials, and lower-secondary school principal talked to us. The principal knew all the answers. But at least the vice mayor took notes, and all seemed interested in what we had to say. . . . In the afternoon, we talked to organization representatives. The *fujinkai* is also the Red Cross volunteer service group— same officers and same members. One fine-looking young man said the *seinendan* tried to use parliamentary procedure, but it was hard to do all at once. What should they start with? I recommended motions because the individual should express his opinion. When we talked about pamphlets, he said people in remote areas do not get them because they cannot attend meetings. That certainly is too bad and probably true. The prefectural people don't make enough effort, I'm afraid.

As soon as possible after meetings ended at three o'clock, we set off on a drive along the coast, headed for Misaki to the CPH we had been scheduled to visit the previous afternoon. Unfortunately, when we reached the town, looking forward to seeing a real CPH building instead of one just on paper, it was locked and barred and no key was available.

The next day, Sunday, we left Shimizu for the drive to Kubokawa. Rather than taking the direct route, at my suggestion we drove around Cape Ashizuri, a place that held a fascination for me because of Manjiro-san. One of the first Japanese in the Tokugawa period to leave the country, return, and not be permanently imprisoned or executed for leaving, Manjiro-san probably was born in 1827 at Nakanohama, a village on the western side of the cape. In those days, a strict policy of isolation kept the Japanese in their country and prohibited foreigners from landing. I wanted in 1950 to stand on the cape in remembrance of when Manjiro-san was not far from there, helpless in a small, disabled fishing boat, facing death at sea or—later—possibly death in

Japan if he returned to Tosa (now Kochi). After he and four other fishermen were blown from near Tosa during a storm, they were finally rescued from a deserted island by an American whaling vessel. Manjiro-san, who became known as John Mungo, landed in 1844 in Fairhaven, Massachusetts, with his rescuer, Captain Whitfield; there, he went to school and learned English. In 1851, he returned to Japan only to be arrested and tried for the crime of leaving the country. Eventually, however, he was allowed to return to Tosa. The Tokugawa government in Tokyo sent for him to interpret in 1853 when Commodore Matthew C. Perry of the U.S. Navy arrived. He accompanied the first Japanese delegation when it sailed to the United States in 1860.

The scenery of the area was another good reason for taking the longer route:

> The view of the Pacific from the end of the cape was magnificent. There was quite some wind, and the waves were white-capped. The sun was shining, the sky was blue, it couldn't have been more beautiful.
>
> As we drove along the shore of the cape, we met many people all dressed up going to local festivals. The vegetation was very different. Subtropical trees grew here, with few pines. The difference in growth was very noticeable. As we got back to the mainland, we found again that everyone was out digging potatoes. There must be billions of them.

Then we discovered that we could not take the road we had expected to travel to Kubokawa through Nakamura: "We had to go way back to Hirata where we had been on the way down. Drove along the same river road for a long time. It added miles and several hours to our trip. So we were especially glad to get to Kubokawa. Our entire trip so far has been either along the sea or in the mountains. Hard on the nerves—but easy on the eyes."

At Kubokawa, "everyone seemed especially anxious to please us. There is a very friendly atmosphere in the inn. Probably not many Americans have been here and no women, we're told. There is a festival in progress—Kompira Festival of Kotohira. As the maid said, 'O-kami-san (the god) visits every shrine, so festivals are held on different days in different places.'"

On Monday morning in Kubokawa, we met with officials and organizations, including the *fujinkai* to which women from Matsubagawa were also invited.

> They came—about fifty strong. They were sorry not all could come, but it is the farming busy season (more sweet potatoes). Their president made a little speech about having been at my meetings since I first was in Kochi and thanked me for all I've done.
>
> We got away after lunch. . . . Began our journey in the mountains. We drove through a little gap, and the most beautiful vista opened. We were high in the mountains. Way below was a little valley with patchwork fields. Far in the distance was the sea. And incredible as it seemed, we ended up at the sea.
>
> [Finally] we rolled into Kochi at five o'clock. It has been a wonderful trip, but I'm glad to be in one piece. Luxury of a heater. And sitting in chairs. And sleeping in a bed.

Looking back on these trips around southern Shikoku, I feel satisfied that I learned many things firsthand that I had suspected before, related to both social education and society in general. Accustomed for many years to following rule from above, people were often puzzled about how to act by themselves. Some looked to those in the occupation force as authorities who could effect changes, even though civil affairs officers only advised the Japanese about their own laws. When people tried to put democratic principles into practice themselves, they sometimes were unsuccessful because they did not really understand what they should do and the reasons for doing so. For example, an American would feel that the inviolability of the secret ballot is of great importance in a democracy. Yet in Mugi, we were asked, "Do you sign your name to a ballot and why not?" Then, in Uwajima, an attempt was made to reach a decision locally about shrine festivals—should the ten continue to be held separately or all on one day? Eighty-nine percent voted for a one-day observance. But after "a few men were very vocal" and because the people did not understand that the majority decision should stand, the question remained unresolved. "Did democracy really work?" they asked. Of course it did; they just did not follow its principles.

I had noted in Muroto that "shoes were removed at this town office before entering." Why did I record such a simple, seemingly unimportant action? Perhaps because this was the only time we left our shoes at the entrance of a government building, and the practice seemed to presage a conservative town administration. However, word must have reached Muroto about the newly mandated equality of women and men, because two young women were among the officials. Although these women were clearly ignorant of what their work was supposed to entail, even the token gesture of having them present to meet an American woman visitor suggested that the officials at least knew what was expected.

Because of the hurried nature of the trips, we had few personal contacts with women. Meeting the widow selling candy drops in Mugi was a reminder that, after the war, many widows were forced to work to support their families in spite of the stigma placed on working women. I felt genuine disappointment not to meet the young woman in Mugi who left a note at the inn after she was too shy to express herself before the group. That she was ready to speak, though too late, was heartening, however. Perhaps another time she had enough courage to voice an opinion or ask a question.

8 · · ·

Four

Women

While my work involved teaching women about democratic political institutions, I could not help being drawn as well into the personal lives of four women who worked closely with me. Through their struggles, I learned how profoundly the family traditions of Japan continued to control their lives—and how hard it was for women to live as individuals within those restrictions.

I got to know Mrs. Teruko Imamura only during the last six months of my stay in Takamatsu, although she had worked in our office for some time. In August 1950, after having been away from the office for a week, she wrote me that her illness might be from a nervous condition. Then she asked if she could talk to me. As a divorced mother who had to work to support her child, she had many worries but no one to talk to: "My minister will scold me, and my friends are too young." Two days later, I stopped at her home to see her, but she was at the hospital, and only her mother and the baby were there. The mother cried at my visit, saying she did not know Americans were so kind.

After Mrs. Imamura returned home from the hospital, I went

to see her and learned that she had had anemia. Then, a few days later, she came with Mrs. Hayashi to the castle:

> Her story is like many others. She is twenty-two, the elder of two daughters, divorced, with a baby almost two. Her father has a small business. Her husband was adopted into the family. Her younger sister is going on to college after high school. Her mother and father want her to stop work and stay home to take care of the baby. She wants to continue work and hire someone to help her mother. . . . She [also] wants to take a course in philosophy from Keio University. But her father says she needs no more education.
>
> She wants to be independent and take care of the baby. She earns some ¥5,000 a month [less than fourteen dollars] so cannot afford to do that. Also, she is a Christian, which apparently does not suit the family. The younger sister seems to do as she likes. On one hand, [Mrs. Imamura] says she feels responsibility to the family as the elder sister. But still she revolts at an aimless life. She fears her father will want her to marry again.

One afternoon three weeks later, Mrs. Imamura came over to bring me a doll she had made for me and to tell me that she had decided to stay at home and take a correspondence course from Keio University. Then, a happy time marked our last meeting when she and her daughter, little Noriko-chan, came with others to the castle to see my Christmas tree. The small guest was entranced by the tiny lights and colored balls. Even now, I can see her as she cautiously approached the tree and touched the balls gently with one finger.

I first met Mrs. Hatsumi Seno in 1947 during the early months of my first winter in Takamatsu. She came into our office from where she worked in the translation section next door, dressed in kimono and with perspiration running down her face, even though it was a cold day and the room was never really warm in winter. I learned that because she had no Western-style clothes, she wore several kimono, as was the custom, to try to keep warm on long train rides in unheated coaches back and forth from her home in the country. Then she was much too warm at the office, wearing all those kimono that were too difficult to remove.

She and I were the same age. After we became acquainted well enough to discuss personal matters, she told me that her father, who was a Buddhist priest, was very understanding. His father had been very strict, and he was determined he would not be that way. When she wanted to be a Christian, he allowed her to go to church; when she wanted to learn English, he gave his permission. Her facility in written English assured her a position as a translator. Because her spoken English was also fine, she sometimes assisted me in interpreting in Takamatsu.

To me, she always seemed to be an old-fashioned woman who found it difficult not to follow the customs of her upbringing. Whenever she came into our office, she bowed at the door — no matter how many times Fred told her, "You don't need to bow when you come in. This is an American office." When she and I walked together on the street, she walked three steps behind me out of respect, until I insisted otherwise.

After we learned that she worked to support an invalid husband and two children, Fred somehow located a house for her in a city where houses were scarce, and she moved her family to Takamatsu. All of us rejoiced that life suddenly became much easier for this woman who worked so hard for her family.

Miss Yoriko Matsumura and I were an unlikely pair: she was small and slight even for a Japanese; I, bulky even for an American. For more than two years as my interpreter, she was my ears and voice when we faced all kinds of situations with a myriad of people and groups. Soon no question arose in my mind that, if in my ignorance I made an inappropriate comment, she would put my English into proper Japanese. One trait we shared was a sense of humor, perhaps the most important of any needed for our travels throughout Shikoku.

During one conversation about education, she reported that a teacher once told her, "This is not a good poem. It is too realistic." When she asked why, the teacher said, "Do not ask such questions." She said that teachers scolded her many times for asking questions, so by the time she got to college, she had learned to keep quiet. When I commented how fortunate it was that at least she had been able to go to college, she replied, "Perhaps that is why I am not happy." I later learned that she'd had two unhappy experiences with marriage. First she fell in love and wanted to marry, but her family did not allow it. Then her family picked a man and she was ready for marriage, but they discovered he was not desirable so that engagement was broken off. By the time I knew her she was nearing the age when Japanese custom dictated she should marry if she was ever going to. However, she told me that she was not interested in marriage and was delighted because her younger sister was going to marry. That the younger sister was to marry even though the elder was not made her feel encouraged that she might not have to marry at all.

Although Miss Matsumura had unconventional attitudes about marriage, her ties to her family were strong. Traditionally, she was never called by her first name at home but always *onesan,* or elder sister—another sign that the individual is less important than the position in the family. Even though she wanted to break away, she felt that she could not, for young women who left home to work seemed less respectable to many Japanese. Still, she wished she could move away from her family, and in May 1949 she asked my opinion about getting a room in Takamatsu. "It is hard to give advice when you know practically everyone is on the other side," I noted in my journal.

On two afternoons in 1949, she, Mrs. Hayashi, and I talked

about marriage and divorce. They asked if I thought Madame
Butterfly was silly because she was faithful to Pinkerton. Then
they told me about a nun who long ago founded a famous nun-
nery that became a sanctuary for women: "If women were
unhappy with their husbands, they went there. If they got even a
clog-length distance from the door, they were safe. After spending three years there, they could leave, remarry, or begin life
again." I learned more about this nun later when I read in *The
Force of Women in Japanese History* a section entitled "A Buddhist
Nun Operates a 'Divorce Temple.'" The nun was Tenshu-ni,
granddaughter of Ieyasu, the first Tokugawa warlord to rule
Japan. This nun, wrote the author,

> operated under the temple creed of the right to divorce
> which the Tokugawa Shogunate legalized by statute, after
> 1600, its dictum reading: "Those who dislike their hus-
> bands and flee to Tokei-ji [the temple] may return to their
> own parents after performing their duties there for three
> years." Thus the approval of the Buddhist Church was
> bestowed upon women who wished to have that religious
> sanction for throwing off the bonds of matrimony.

I met Miss Matsumura's parents in July 1949, after she telephoned to say she could not come in to the office because she had
a bad case of athlete's foot. I felt responsible because she very
likely had picked up this malady on a field trip with me, so I
decided to take her some medicine. On the following day, Saturday, Mrs. Hayashi and I drove to the Matsumura home, where I
found that the family lived at the back of the store owned by her
father. Miss Matsumura was dressed for company, so I presumed
she was expecting us. Mr. Matsumura took Mrs. Hayashi, Miss
Matsumura, and me upstairs in the store to the third-floor tea
room: "We three sat down. Soon came cider, peaches, a small
melon, and finally watermelon. Mrs. Matsumura appeared,

dressed in sheer kimono. She didn't want to stay, as she is shy, but we finally prevailed upon her to do so."

In an attempt to help Miss Matsumura become trained in office procedures, I talked to her in July 1949 about how I scheduled field trips and showed her my notes. She brought back the typed plans, saying she would not have thought to do some of the things I had put on the paper. She repeated the common phrase, "It is so scientific." By December, she had worked out a schedule for our January and February trips, but told me it had been difficult because she had not done it before and "my mind is not systematic." At another time when we were discussing plans, she said, "I have no opinion. When you ask for my opinion, I have none." Then in March 1950, I had the opportunity to take a three-week holiday, but we still needed to visit Ehime and Tokushima to keep to our planned schedule. I talked the situation over with Miss Matsumura, and we decided that she would go to Ehime and Tokushima on her own. When I announced the decision at a civil education staff meeting, I called her "Matsumura-joshi" (learned woman). When I asked if she had anything to add, she said that if we were Japanese officials, we would never send her off on field trips because she was young. She knew we wanted her to go because it would be a good experience for her and because we didn't want the program interrupted, but she felt nervous about it, saying, "I am a miserable joshi."

Once, she said she could not remember when Japan was not at war. During World War II, she said, she was always hungry. The people were told to exercise, she said; then they would forget their hunger. Although we seldom discussed relationships between Japanese and Americans, on a trip in Tokushima she said something about racial prejudice. I said I didn't believe that I had any toward the Japanese. She admitted that she thought Fred and I were not prejudiced. I said many Americans were not. I told her that, if she visited my family, they would treat her the same way they would any of my friends. I had a chance to say later that I knew the Japanese had been told by their leaders that Americans thought the Japanese were an inferior race, but I asked her to remember that such an idea was nonsense as far as I was concerned.

When Miss Matsumura and I traveled during the winter, we often were cold. Once when we commiserated about the difficulty of getting to sleep when our feet were cold, I told her that, even if I could not take a bath, I would warm my feet in hot water just before getting into a chilly bed. She remarked that often she did not want to use the bath in an inn because, as a woman, her turn was always last and then the water was the least clean. Then I asked if she could not obtain from the kitchen enough hot water to warm her feet. That was not possible, she said. "Could you get hot tea?" was my next question. "Of course, always." "Then why don't you ask for tea and warm your feet in it?" After she got over the first shock of this unconventional idea, she agreed to try it and pronounced herself satisfied with the results. But when she told her family what she did, they indicated their disapproval and so she discontinued the hot-tea footbaths.

It was on a field trip to Tokushima that I first became aware of the standards of propriety Japanese women kept in the company of other women. Miss Matsumura went with me to my room late in the afternoon while we waited for a jeep to pick her up to take her to the inn where she was staying:

> I asked if she would like to lie down. She did but kept on her dress. When I suggested she take it off rather than wrinkle it, she said she had been taught never to undress in front of anyone else — not even her parents. I replied that was silly in my opinion and that she had seen me in my slip the day before. So I left the room ostensibly to wash my hands but primarily to give her a chance to take off her dress if she wanted to. When I returned, she had done so.

I asked if she had been taught that in school. Yes, [she said]
in the dormitory everyone was that way. So I tried to say
one could be a lady and modest without false modesty.

On later occasions when we were on The Eagle and got ready for
bed in the coach, she put a loose sleeping kimono over her slip
and undressed and dressed under it. As I look back now on our
trips together, I wonder if such intimate relations between a
young woman and her older American supervisor were more
distressing to her than I ever suspected.

A few weeks before I departed Takamatsu, Mrs. Hayashi told
me that Miss Matsumura might get married. Apparently she and
the man had their first "interview." I noted, "I'm sorry to hear
this, in a way. But perhaps it is the best, considering Japan and
the way people think."

I met Mrs. Sumiko Hayashi soon after I arrived on Shikoku,
when she attended the meeting for women who spoke English at
the time we were looking for an interpreter. She told me long
afterwards, "When I got the card from the prefecture and the
military government saying I was to go to a meeting, I did not
want to go. My mother said I should go or they would scold me.
But the last morning, I decided to go. I could not imagine there
would be a woman in military government." About a month
later, she came from the nearby city where she lived to our office
looking for a job. Her English wasn't good enough for a job as an
interpreter, but I was impressed with her and gave her another
position. I have no idea what the title was in the records, but I
considered her my assistant.

Often she told me long after an event what her feelings had
been at the time. Once, for example, after a meeting with several men officials and before she and I went to our next appointment with other men, I asked her if she would like to go to the
ladies' room. She acquiesced immediately, and I led the way to a

row of outdoor toilets, one designated for women. Later she told me that when I had asked my question, she thought, "We've been talking to men all morning, and it would be nice to see some women." She had been disappointed to discover that the "ladies' room" was just the toilet.

For some time, she was an observer at meetings I conducted, but gradually she became more knowledgeable until later she made field trips alone. I was initially surprised that she agreed to travel by herself around the island, since traveling alone was so unconventional for a Japanese woman. However, her only un-pleasant experience of which I was aware involved a captain on the regional staff. I described the incident in my journal: "Mrs. Hayashi came to tell me the captain (the skunk) had been chasing her—figuratively and otherwise. She was concerned lest I tell him where she now lives. It goes way back almost a year, I think. In February he drove her home from the ferry when she came back from Tokyo. He was in Tokushima a couple of times when she was. The last time she asked him [how he knew she was there], and he said he looked on the calendar to see her sched-ule." This calendar, upon which we all recorded field trips, hung in the civil education office. When I discussed the situa-tion with Fred, he was as furious with the captain as I was. We had no more trouble, however, after we started recording Mrs. Hayashi's trips in the wrong prefecture and the captain was hood-winked.

As time passed, Mrs. Hayashi became increasingly helpful in our work with women. After additional fields of interest were added to my responsibilities, I found she could assist me greatly with religion, arts, and monuments. She suggested I read about Buddhism to help me understand the Japanese, saying that her understanding of Americans had been helped by reading about Christianity. One shared cultural experience, unforgettable for both of us, was when we visited the Shosoin, a treasure-house near the Todai-ji, the Buddhist temple in Nara that held the

Great Buddha. I had been fascinated when I first read of the ancient storehouse that contained valuables and antiques, mostly of the eighth century, but was disappointed to read in an old guidebook, "The Shosoin is not open to the general public, only Japanese of high rank being admitted to inspect the treasures." Undeterred by these obstacles, I requested and received an invitation from the Imperial Household, through the civil affairs team in Nara, to visit the Shosoin during the airing of its treasures in October 1949. Mrs. Hayashi happily consented to accompany me.

The gate in the wall surrounding the treasure-house was opened at ten o'clock on October 29, and a sergeant and his wife, a single woman, and I were the first Americans. We had to sign a book before entering. Mrs. Hayashi was the first to sign one for the Japanese: "I thought we were never going to get past that book, as she hesitated to sign. Here she was a woman—not an 'important person'—and the first. But she finally got it done after much talking to the official."

On the following day, she wanted me to see clay figures of the Tempyo period (eighth century) in a small hall near the Shosoin that was not open to the public. Her friend who was with us left to seek permission for our entry; soon he returned with a slip for "Jonson-san, Takamatsu Minjibu" (civil affairs section) that allowed us to enter. These two incidents illustrated two sides of Mrs. Hayashi. In the first, she found it very difficult to sign the guest book when her name would appear first of the many Japanese who would sign. But in the second, she took the initiative to ask for a privilege that I would not have requested, even if I'd been aware of the valued art objects we wished to see.

Once when our conversation turned to racial and national differences, she said that "she could not be proud of Japan. Then I said every country does things of which it later is not proud: Nanking by the Japanese—the German treatment of the Jews—our treatment of *nisei* and their parents in World War II. But we cannot blame a whole nation for what a few bad leaders did. I cited the industry and honesty of the Japanese as an illustration. 'Oh, Miss Johnson, you are looking at only the good things in Japan.'"

After I returned home, I assembled little bits of my journal to create a record of Mrs. Hayashi's life before and during the war and while her country was occupied. (Although I sometimes referred to her in my journal as Sumiko, I would never have called her that in person, as it would have violated Japanese standards of politeness.) Her early life was spent in a city near Takamatsu where her mother's merchant-class family had lived for generations. In the absence of a male heir, her father had been adopted into the family and assumed its name. Even though she attended college in Tokyo at "a school quite revolutionary for the times," the instruction was formal, and independent thinking discouraged. She remembered her principal once saying, "When you travel in trains, everyone [Japanese] is reading. Foreigners, on the other hand, do not read like that on the train. They look out the window, make notes of what they see, walk about the platform when the train stops. But when you asked a Japanese what he thinks, he said, 'Goethe says. . . . Tolstoi says. . . . Dostoevski says. . . .' He has no opinions of his own."

Mrs. Hayashi's father attended her graduation and wanted her to return home, but she did not want to. When he asked for a reason, she gave him an unimportant one because she had never confided in him. But he told her he wanted her to return for a Buddhist festival, and she finally acquiesced. On her return, the family decided that she should remain at home, but her problems with her father continued:

> One day she told her father he did not love her nor the family. "He was going to strike me and took hold of my arm. Many servants rushed in to stop him. My mother came and took his fingers off one by one. (She illustrated

how the fingers had been pried off.) I could not stay in my house so I left for five days and stayed with my friend. I went to a temple to see the priest. He was a philosopher as well as a priest. Then my father became very ill, about to die. I went into the room where he was lying. My heart became free." This all is not too clear to me as I try to write it down. But I think she meant to say she forgave him and then felt all was well.

Mrs. Hayashi, a widow when I knew her, had met her husband at college. Her parents did not want her to marry him, since he was in the movie business. But if he would give up his work and go into business with her father, they would agree to let the couple marry. Her friends thought she was in love to want to marry someone of whom her parents did not approve. But she says she does not think she was: she just wanted to get away from her family—and he from his. When I asked if she was happy in her marriage, she paused and then said yes. She told me of one time when they both received invitations to a college reunion and she said she was too busy to go. He said, "I did not marry you for you to be always washing." She said that kind of conversation occurred many times.

Early in 1945, their house in Tokyo was bombed and burned, and she brought her son, then a toddler, back to her parents' home on Shikoku. Then in July, Shikoku was bombed. She received news that her husband in Tokyo was dying, but she could not go to him; there were no ferries because Takamatsu had been hit.

As a widow, Mrs. Hayashi was no longer called by her married name of Sumiko Nishi; her name was removed from the Nishi family register and added to the Hayashi register as Sumiko Hayashi. Her baby, Ichiro-chan, retained the Nishi name, as the eldest son of the eldest son of the family. The mother-in-law came to Shikoku to see the baby and decided to stay, because her

eldest son and her husband were dead and she had no more ties
in Tokyo. But it was difficult all living together, so Mrs. Hayashi
got a house in the country nearby for mother-in-law, the baby,
and a servant. When her brother-in-law came back from Russia
in the early part of 1948,

> he went to the Hayashi home where his mother was. He
> blames Sumiko for not telling him about the father's and
> elder brother's deaths, burning of the house, and birth of
> Ichiro. But his mother talked to him all night the first
> night, telling him her side of the story.

Not long afterward, when Mrs. Hayashi came to the military
government meeting for women who spoke English, a terrible
thing happened. While she was gone, the mother-in-law took
the baby and went back to Tokyo. According to Japanese custom,
Ichiro-chan, son of the eldest son, was considered head of the
Nishi family, but I considered her action an incredibly cruel thing
to do to her daughter-in-law. In fact, Mrs. Hayashi's brother-in-
law's friends had told him he must not let his mother take the boy
without telling her daughter-in-law, but he did nothing to stop
his mother. The mother-in-law then said that Mrs. Hayashi was
not a good mother because she did not go right to Tokyo after
her baby. I felt that was certainly unfair. Her accusation, however, worried Mrs. Hayashi, and she asked me if I thought she
was a bad mother because of that. How could an American
answer that? All I could say was that I, knowing the family system
and the Japanese, did not think it strange that she did as she did.
Unfortunately, Mrs. Hayashi's problem was compounded by the
attitude of her own parents, who never approved of her working.
Four months after she joined the civil education staff, she confided to me that her family wished her to marry again. Her family home was to be sold—unless she remarried. I wondered at
the time if she was going to be brave enough to resist her family's
wishes.

A year after she began work in our office, she attended a conference in Tokyo and attempted to see Ichiro-chan, then six years old, but failed. About a month later, she brought her mother to the office; apparently she wanted her mother and the Americans to meet. That relations between mother and daughter were not close may be surmised from a story she told me. She was walking near her home when she met a former maid from her family's household. The woman had lost her husband a few months before and had a nine-month-old baby. "I know it was impolite," Mrs. Hayashi said, "but I took all my money and gave it to her. I thought when I got home, I would borrow from my mother, but when I got there, I was ashamed. I knew if I needed money, I could borrow from you. Isn't it funny that I would be ashamed to borrow from my mother but not from you?"

Some time in June 1949, Mrs. Hayashi left the family home to live with an aunt in Takamatsu. She spoke of the family home that month when she told me about the spirit or ghost seen by a woman servant: "It walked 'like a pussy cat' and had no arms or legs. The servant asked if it wanted to speak 'to the madam,' but it evidently did not. She said her family did not mind living with a ghost. The ghost appears in the Buddhist niche or place of worship." Five days later, she commented, "The ghost is the spirit of someone who once lived there long ago. It never speaks. I asked if she had ever seen it. She said no but that she had felt it."

On the Saturday in the following month when she and I took medicine to Miss Matsumura at her home, we also went to the Hayashi home. After entering through their dressmaking shop, we went upstairs, around corners, and down long halls until we came to a Western-style room with chairs and a davenport covered in white cloth. Mrs. Hayashi wanted me to see the Buddhist shrine. All the usual Buddhist accessories and hangings were present, along with a lovely carved Kannon (a god of mercy) in honor of the aunt's deceased husband—a general. She told me that it was in this room that the spirit appears. Soon Mr. Hayashi arrived, and we had formal tea in the ceremonial tea room. Mrs. Hayashi then wanted me to see the Japanese room—two large rooms long and narrow. In a conspicuous place was a fan-shaped, glass base upon which rested two lovely blue china or glass carp. She said the carp were in honor of her marriage. Mrs. Hayashi seemed to think the house was a sad place, dark and foreboding. I thought the Buddhist shrine must have a great influence on the whole family. I had felt a materialistic air at the Matsumuras' because we talked in the store; at the Hayashis' house, I felt old Japanese feudalism.

At the door when we left was an old woman, evidently a servant. On the way home, Mrs. Hayashi said the old woman always asked about her little boy. Her family, she added, never did. I said I never did, not because I had forgotten, but because it might make her sad to talk about him. She said, "Oh, no."

Later we talked more about the spirit. Mrs. Hayashi said that her mother had been looking at the old family records once when she found a name of another child born on the same day as herself. But "old people have prejudices against twins," she said, so her mother did not want the fact known. The mother decided to have a private ceremony for the spirit at a certain time. But then the eldest son died, and the ceremony was not held. So she thought the ghost might be the spirit of her mother's twin that was coming back. "When did he die?" I asked. "I think when he was born."

Mrs. Hayashi's plans progressed, and by August 8, 1949, she was ready to "borrow" a house so that she could bring her boy to live with her in Takamatsu. On Sunday, August 21, I noted in my journal, "Mrs. Hayashi goes to Tokyo today to get her little boy." Then, on the following Friday evening, she called from Uno, across the Inland Sea, about eight o'clock to say she would arrive in Takamatsu about eleven. "I did not bring my boy," she said. I found a friend with a jeep to pick her up. She looked tired and pale, and of course she wept. I felt terribly sorry for her but was not too surprised, feeling she just wasn't strong enough to buck her in-laws.

[The next day] Mrs. Hayashi came about two o'clock. . . . "My mother-in-law is a strong-willed woman," she began. I tried to do little but listen until she had said all she wanted to. She was promised by her brother-in-law (without her mother-in-law's knowledge) that she can have Ichiro-chan in six months. I asked her if she believed that. "Yes." "Are you satisfied with this answer?" "Yes." "Then I'm satisfied, too." In this six-month period, the mother-in-law is to be persuaded to let the boy go. Only the actual event in six months will prove that to me!

Under the old family system, the eldest son of the eldest son must be taken care of by the brothers, his uncles. Therefore, Mrs. Hayashi's brother-in-law was responsible for Ichiro-chan. The house the family lived in, however, was too small, so they moved into a doctor's house. The doctor, who lived in a little house nearby, had a daughter of twenty and two small children but no wife. So it was planned that the brother-in-law would marry the daughter and they could live permanently in the house. He would do all this to provide for Ichiro-chan. However, if Mrs. Hayashi were to take her boy, the brother-in-law would not need to "marry a place to live."

One more angle on the Hayashi family. The eldest son had become an architect and had not followed the family business. Mrs. Hayashi's husband worked two years in Shanghai for the family, but then went on to his own living. Then when the younger sister was to be married, her father wanted to adopt the husband into the family. Mrs. Hayashi's husband told him something about what that would mean. When the younger sister's fiancé finally refused, Mrs. Hayashi's husband was blamed. Mrs.

Hayashi herself was blamed for another family "loss" because she was supposed to have influenced the youngest son to study literature instead of going into the family business.

One day, in the midst of all the trouble about her son and her in-laws, I asked Mrs. Hayashi if she had slept well the previous night. "Yes," she said, "I took some medicine." That led to the fact that, while in Tokyo, she had slept little and was very sad. For the trip back, she took some sleeping medicine, but her younger brother did not know that. When he got off the train in Kobe, he shook her; but that was all she remembered until she was in Hiroshima, past where she should have gotten off. That was why she was so late getting back that night. I asked her not to use the sleeping medicine any more. She said she had bought enough to kill herself. "Suicide is a cowardly thing," I said. "It means you cannot face life." "I cannot believe I am independent," she said. I hoped that my being there helped give her courage to become stronger and independent of her family so that she could make a home for her boy. Three days later, I recorded, "She has stopped taking the medicine."

In October 1949, a conference of regional civil education officers took me to Yokohama. When I returned, Mrs. Hayashi told me:

> Her family wants her to marry. She cannot make them understand that she does not want to. She does not think a husband and Ichiro-chan could go together. They have the man all picked out. While I was gone, they persuaded her to come home. She could not fight against them, she said. The mother of the man was to come to talk it over. I think she has promised to see him and perhaps consider the idea. This she did only to satisfy her parents, I think.
>
> They are concerned about her future. It is understandable to me but still does not help matters any. I asked her what she would like to do if she could decide. She wants to

work and take care of Ichiro-chan. I tried to make her see that we [occupation officials] are here for only a time and that perhaps she should get a permanent job. But she doesn't want to do that. So all I can do, I guess, is to give her moral support and not let her feel too discouraged. She seems to feel she just cannot get away from her family. Poor dear. Life is certainly hard for her.

Mrs. Hayashi was ill and at home off and on from January through March 1950. After her first two days of absence with a cold, I went to see her and found that her room was freezing, so I bought a heater and sent it to her. On one of my visits during her illness, she told me her father said to the young woman who lives with them that, when he turned the corner toward her house, he felt ashamed for himself and the family that she was living there alone. She returned to the office early in February, but again became ill. After being out for a week, she persuaded the doctor to say she should be out five days instead of seven: "Yesterday I put my foot down and said she must stay out until she was well. Today (when she was supposed to be back) she sent over two rice cakes for each of us—one white and one pink. Mrs. Inagaki said that is customary when people return to work after an illness." When she did come back to work, her schedule was curtailed on orders from her doctor, and she could not go on field trips: "But then it all came out that she was afraid she would be fired. Next, she said she must decide soon about Ichiro-chan. She can either bring him here or go to Tokyo."

Her health was still not good, and she was out the whole next month. Before the end of that time, however, she told me of her desire to go to Tokyo to work; her brother-in-law had written that Ichiro-chan had had his examination for school, and she took this news as proof that they didn't intend to let him go. Then two days later, she wrote me she was going to stay in the office. After I returned from a three-week holiday in Hong Kong and Thailand, I noted in my journal, "Mrs. Hayashi is in Tokyo. Why? I don't know." My question was answered three days later: "Mrs. Hayashi back to work. And she brought Ichiro-chan back with her. I never thought she would do that. She stole him away. He has no clothes, no registration card, no ration card. I only hope the family does not do anything to hurt her and him." Her action was legal under the new laws of Japan, but she was confronting traditions that were still strong.

A week later, she came to the castle to say she was "worried about Ichiro-chan. He likes living with his mother but doesn't like school. He is happy and 'full of spirits' in school but cries during free play. I think he is finding it hard to adjust to all the new children, whom he can hardly understand because of the difference in speech." On the following Wednesday afternoon, they came to call: "He certainly is a bright little boy. He brought an alphabet book (from the American CI&E library). He knew almost all the objects in English. Even his mother was surprised."

At the office the following day, Mrs. Hayashi told me that she was trying to get a copy of the register from Tokyo so she could get Ichiro-chan properly tended to. All the records in the ward where she was registered were burned during the war. The Nishis had reregistered the family, neglecting to say that she was his mother. She said she was "shocked," as she had trusted her brother-in-law. I was not surprised. Now she would have to get verification that she married her husband, to prove that she was Ichiro-chan's mother. I asked her if she needed anything. She hesitated, then said she had only one shirt for Ichiro-chan, which she washed every night: "I sent her off to buy another shirt. Cost ¥245 (about seventy cents). She said she had money enough to eat but not enough till pay day for the shirt. I gave her ¥2,000 (about $5.50) the other day. But half she sent to Tokyo because she had borrowed ¥1,000 from a friend. Bless her heart. She does have courage."

At another time, Ichiro-chan helped me celebrate Tanabata,

or the weavers' festival, held on the seventh day of the seventh month, when the Weaver Maiden (the star Vega) and the Herd-boy (the star Altair) meet this one day of the year in the Milky Way. Ichiro-chan "brought me a little willow branch decorated with bits of paper. In olden times, branches would be set afloat the next morning, I'm told." And I can still see in my mind's eye one day when Ichiro-chan marched up to my desk after lunch and began "*Obachama* (Aunt), Mama-san . . ." as he explained that his mother was not feeling well and would not return to the office for the afternoon.

For the winter, I ordered Ichiro-chan some warm clothes from a Chicago department store: coat, ski pants, cap, shoes, mittens, socks, sweater, and white shirt. On the night the clothes arrived, he insisted on taking his new shoes to bed with him.

In January 1951, just before my colleague Bernard Dobbins and I left Shikoku, "the office staff had a party for Dobbie and me. Sandwiches, coffee, and cake were served. Then we had 'recreation.' Almost everyone did something for the entertainment. It was very nice! Mrs. Hayashi read a little speech of thanks for the closing. No gifts. No tears."

That Mrs. Hayashi was chosen to speak for a staff of men and women, some of whom were her elders, seems more significant now than it did then. In Japanese circles, this could have meant that she—a woman—was considered the most important person on the staff to speak for all. In another indication of her growing independence, "A few days later, Mrs. Hayashi and I had a chance to talk by ourselves. She plans to work in the prefectural library after civil affairs closes. I think that is a good place for her. She had been undecided about staying at the office, but the final journey around the island led to her resolve to stay. [She said,] 'The women need me.'"

After World War II and the adoption of a new constitution and legal system, many Japanese women worked who, in prewar times, would have married and remained in the home. Some were forced to turn to business because they were widowed or were supporting invalid husbands. Others wished to be independent. The four in this chapter needed to work or wished to do so, even though marriage and home life were still considered more desirable by most Japanese. Only a woman who faced two opposing courses could know how difficult was the choice she must make between following traditions and breaking them. To be independent, she must be willing to defy custom and face censure by her family and society.

Added to the stigma of working were other obstacles: women's inferior education; respect for elders because age presumably brought wisdom; docility toward men; no experience in office work; and absence of qualifications such as initiative that were necessary for advancement in business but undesirable in Japanese women. But by far the most significant aspect of the conflict for women was rooted in two related concepts: filial piety and the family system. Closely related were conflicts about marriage. Provisions in the new constitution that "marriage shall be based on the mutual consent of both sexes" implied some personal choice for young people instead of only arrangements made by two families, usually through a go-between. In spite of this change, the parents of Mrs. Hayashi and Miss Matsumura took preliminary steps to arrange marriages against the wishes of their daughters. Mrs. Imamura's position was further complicated by the ancient custom that obligated a family to have a male heir. After her marriage to a man adopted into her family failed and ended in divorce, she feared that her father would want her to remarry to carry on the family name.

Then, as now, I deplored precepts that placed so little value on the individual and demanded compliance with the family system. Then, as now, I feel only regret that efforts to achieve independence caused so much unhappiness for these women who were so courageous and for whom I cared so much.

My journal pages are blank, and so is my memory, about what took place between the final entry on February 3, 1951—"the die is cast; we leave by plane on February 25 for Hong Kong and points west"—and February 19 when the ferry carried me on the first lap of my journey back to the United States. Was the Takamatsu police band at the dock to play its customary rendition of "Auld Lang Syne" for departing Americans? Did those on the dock throw confetti to the upper deck as the ferry pulled out? Who was there to say good-bye?

All I remember is that Miss Matsumura, Mrs. Hayashi, and Ichiro-chan rode with me to Uno, where we said good-bye, and that we all cried. After I debarked and found an end seat on the train to Okayama, I made an effort to eat the lunch someone had given me. I tried not to break down again, thinking that I would probably never see those friends again.

My few days in Tokyo were filled with last-minute arrangements for the trip home. I also attended, with two friends, *kabuki* in its new theater. The traditional Japanese occasion could not have been more suitable for a sentimental American woman leaving the country she had come to love.

Afterward, one of my companions, without explanation, drove her car to the outskirts of the city and pointed to the view in the distance. From that vantage point, I had my final view in the gorgeous gold sunset of snow-covered Fuji-san looming out of the sky.

Epilogue · · ·

Throughout the occupation years, my goals remained constant: to do what I could to help the people of Japan make their transition to democracy and to help the women achieve equality as guaranteed by law. Curiosity may have led me to that country, but the desire to assist women was the reason for my long stay. Even in my early months in Nagoya, however, I became aware of the many obstacles to democracy facing the Japanese people, and I was often perplexed about what to suggest in difficult situations. I began to question how I, with my American background, could—or should—counsel Japanese women who sought my advice. As my understanding increased with the passage of time, so did my realization of the differences between the two countries.

Despite my doubts, I left the country with a sense of achievement regarding my goals and a warm feeling toward the people, especially the women, with whom I had worked. I also felt gratitude that I was a part of an important episode in history. Without any doubt, the years I spent in Japan were the most exciting and rewarding of my life.

Fortunately, my return to the United States in 1951 was not the end of my interest in and connections with Japan and its people. For my master's degree in adult education from the University of Chicago, I completed several class assignments and a master's paper about the education of women in Japan. There, I was delighted to meet again Mrs. Kimi Hara, former director of the Japanese Girl Scouts, and I became close friends with Mr. Tokuo Akatsuka, a fellow student. I renewed my friendship with Marie Gagner Truax, another former women's affairs officer, living nearby.

For a few years, I tried to keep informed about what was taking place in Japan through a subscription to the *Nippon Times*, but I had to cancel my subscription when I accepted a demanding position in Washington, D.C., as executive director of Pi Lambda Theta, a national honor and professional association for women in education. I then held a position as a writer-editor with the federal government until my retirement. In 1975, my brother, his wife, and I visited Japan, chiefly to help celebrate the 100th anniversary of the founding of Kobe College for young women, but also for brief visits to Kyoto, Nara, Takamatsu, and Tokushima. In 1978, a University of Maryland researcher interviewed me about my years in Japan for the university's oral history archive.

I presented papers related to my occupation experience at a number of conferences, including five symposiums at the MacArthur Memorial Foundation in Norfolk, Virginia, and in 1980 at the Mid-Atlantic Region of the Association for Asian Studies at the University of Maryland. I attended the "We the People" conference commemorating the fortieth anniversary of the new Japanese constitution, also at the University of Maryland. And over the years, I have continued to read books and other materials about Japan, attend Japanese performances and exhibits, and keep in touch with friends from Japan.

In 1986, parts of a manuscript I wrote in the early 1980s were published in Japanese by Domes Publications in Tokyo under the title *Senryo Nikki: Kusanone no Onna Tachi* (Occupation Journal: Women at the Grassroots). Because that publication made my name and whereabouts known in Japan, my experience as a former occupation official became part of a thirty-minute documentary shown on Japanese television in 1991. The producers interviewed me in my apartment and borrowed an episode in my story for the documentary's title: *Oito Yobareru Onna Tachi: Kiroku ni Nihon Josei* (Women Called "*Oi!*": A Historical Look at Japanese Women).

Long after my departure from Japan, I finally was able to learn more about another problem of discrimination that I had heard of during the occupation but about which I could do little at the time. In ancient days, the people who formed the lowest social class in Japan were called *eta,* "people of filth." They are now known as *burakumin* (people of the special section), a word that I never heard or read until I saw it in a book published in 1978. Before the Meiji Restoration in 1868, the population was divided rigidly into social classes: warriors at the top, followed by farmers, artisans, and merchants. Below all were the *burakumin*. Because Buddhism, which played an important part in the history of Japan, forbids the killing of animals, those engaged in work such as butchering or tanning formed this lowest caste. Members of this group were not allowed to mix with or marry individuals from other classes.

After the Meiji Restoration, Japan's first constitution eliminated strict class divisions, and the ancient word *eta* was abolished from the language. Members of that group, however, were still limited to certain professions. Then, after World War II, Article 14 of the new constitution provided legal grounds for equality of all people: there should be "no discrimination in political, economic, or social relations, because of race, creed, sex, social status or family origin." But even then, the word's connotations remained known, and social prejudice and discrimination against the group continued to flourish.

When I was on Shikoku from 1947 to 1951, I saw evidence that discrimination still existed against the *burakumin*. Considering the increased mobility and decreased attention to class in the postwar years, one may wonder how such discrimination could continue when a member of that group could simply move to a large city and be lost in the crowd. The answer lay in family records kept by the government showing ancestors and their origins.

In November 1948, on a trip with Fred Kerlinger, I had my first contact with *burakumin* when we visited a village near Takamatsu. My initial impressions were of the dirtiness of where they lived and the surprising rudeness of the people. Almost two years later, in August 1950, on a regular field trip to Tokushima, I was asked to meet with the Dowakai (Harmony Association), an organization of *burakumin* and people trying to help them. That meeting turned out to be informative but very frustrating for me, because there was little I could do except listen to their story and express my sympathy for their efforts.

I unexpectedly came to understand the degree of prejudice towards these people when first writing about my experiences in the early 1980s. When I sent sections of my manuscript to friends in Japan for their comments, I was surprised when they advised me to delete all references to the *burakumin* (essentially the information in the preceding two paragraphs). My friends felt that retaining that information would prevent the publication of *Senryo Nikki*. Knowing this was a real possibility, I agreed to keep only a brief statement in the manuscript.

Shortly after the book became available in Japan, I received a letter from Mr. Toshio Watanabe of the Buraku Liberation Research Institute (Buraku Kaiho Kenkyusho) in Osaka. He asked if I had information about the *burakumin* beyond the brief mention in the book. I sent him the deleted parts of my manuscript, which he included in a volume published by the institute.

Mr. Watanabe and I kept up our correspondence after this episode, and we finally met when he and his niece visited Washington in March 1989. At that time, I was able to give him a document that I knew would be of great value to him. Years earlier when I began research about *burakumin*, I had written to American friends who might have pertinent material from their time in Japan during the occupation. No one had found anything at the time. But, two months before Mr. Watanabe's visit, I had received a mimeographed copy of a ten-page, single-spaced, typed report from Dobbie, then living in California. The report, which had just turned up in his files, was "The Present Situation of *Eta* (or *Etta*) in Shikoku," dated 10 October 1950 and prepared by Mr. Masao Wada, a scholar and historian who had been on our civil education staff. At the top of the first page was "Mr. Dobbins" in my handwriting. Mr. Wada must have written the report at my request before my meeting in Tokushima. We had both forgotten about the document and had no idea where the original might be. Mr. Watanabe was thrilled to receive this paper, because members of his institute were eager for any material related to the *burakumin* during the occupation.

Mr. Watanabe's visit to my apartment was extremely pleasant, and we discovered that his mother and I were the same age— then 79. When he stood beside me for a picture, I heard him say quietly to himself, "My mothah." His letters after his return to Japan began to use the salutation, "Dear My Mother, Miss Johnson." They still do. When I wrote, "Does your mother know you have a second mother in the United States?" his reply was, "She thinks I am a lucky boy to have two mothers." This may have suggested to me that we use first names; he never does, but I began to call him Toshio.

In 1992, Toshio wrote to invite me to visit Osaka. "If you come to Japan," he urged, "I will introduce you my wife, my mother in Japan, a mother of my wife, a mother of my brother's wife, and many other mothers." During my trip to Osaka in May 1993, I did meet all those mothers. To my delight, I also saw Mr. Kyo Funaki, my star pupil in my English class for businessmen; he journeyed from nearby Nagoya to see me.

A good bit of my time during that trip was spent on activities related to *burakumin*. One day, we went to a branch office of the Buraku Liberation League. Mr. Tanaka, the head, showed us a progressive series of blown-up aerial photographs illustrating how crowded neighborhoods were being replaced by better housing, and paths only wide enough for a cart by wide roads. Mr. Tanaka then drove us through the *buraku* to see present conditions, including some public housing. The next morning, we visited Osaka's Museum of Liberty, which is devoted to the subject of human rights. There were displays on *burakumin*, Koreans, Japanese poisoned by mercury, those who suffered under the Nazis (with a picture of Anne Frank), and Hiroshima. I was particularly interested in another display—this one on black people—for we had eaten dinner one night with a couple and their son who had formed the Association to Stop Racism Against Blacks after the son became concerned by seeing in stores dolls and toys that caricatured blacks.

At the Buraku Liberation Research Institute, Toshio's organization, we had one meeting with some twenty men and women on the staff and another meeting with ten women to discuss my experience during the war and the occupation. During a two-day side trip to Kochi City on Shikoku, I renewed acquaintance with a Girl Scout leader I'd known during the occupation, and was driven around the city but saw little that was familiar. I also met Mrs. Junko Ikegawa, the translator of *Senryo Nikki*. Back in the mid-1980s, she had sent me an English translation of her epilogue to the book, and I had discovered an amazing coincidence. As a teenager in wartime Japan, she had helped to make the "balloon bombs" sent over the Pacific to the United States. One of my jobs as a U.S. combat intelligence officer during the war had been to track the discovery of those bombs and the damage they caused.

In May 1995, around the time of my eighty-fifth birthday, I visited Japan again, this time as the guest of Shikoku Broadcasting Television, which was developing a series on the fiftieth anniversary of World War II, including a documentary about my role in the occupation called *Misu Jonson no Mita Yume: Sengo Kakumei to Awajo Tachi* (Miss Johnson's Dream: Postwar Reform and the Women of Awa [former name of Tokushima]).

My time was filled with interviews, meetings, and activities (most filmed at least twice). A joyous ceremony with 120 Girl Scouts in blue uniforms was followed by ceremonial tea with scout leaders, including an eighty-six-year-old who had been trained by me. She says in the documentary, "Miss Johnson brought with her a feeling of America. Right after the war, we were all hesitating for a moment in shock, and she brought life and energy to us." Toshio Watanabe, my Japanese "son," came from Osaka for dinner the day before Mother's Day, presenting me with three red carnations: one from his mother, one from his wife's mother, and one from him. One morning was spent with members of a women's organization, Akebono-kai (Light of Dawn), which had been formed by prominent Tokushima women in June 1946; some of them remembered meetings with me during the occupation.

Another day we visited Tada House, where I had stayed during my first weeks on Shikoku. Mr. Tada, a gentleman of the old school, greeted us and served ceremonial tea at a small table and benches in the garden. He talked about the presence of American troops on the estate during the occupation and told us his father had been given twenty-four hours to remove everything from the house. His father replied, "America is not yet two hundred years old, but this house is three hundred years old." Then he was told he could have forty-eight hours. Mr. Tada said his family was apprehensive at first about what the Americans might do, but he now only remembered their being "friendly and kind."

Perhaps the best part of my visit was my reunion with one old friend and meeting the daughter of another. Midori Bando Sakai, whom I'd always known as Annie, had been my interpreter during the first part of my stay on Shikoku and my good friend from that time on. Our meetings since 1951 had been brief—a few times when she visited the United States and in 1975 when I was in Tokyo. Finally, with more time to talk, we immediately resumed our friendship, and Annie interpreted for the balance of my trip. I had also been close to Mrs. Harue Kushi during the occupation when she was the prefectural official who worked with women. Mrs. Kushi had died some years earlier, but her daughter, Mrs. Hiroko Kondo, stayed with me for most of this trip. We exchanged many stories about her mother, and she shared with me pictures her mother had saved of our time together during the occupation.

Several months after returning home to Washington, I received a videotape of the documentary with the script summarized in English. Watching it brought back memories of the good work and good friends that Japan has now meant to me for a big part of my life. Near the end of the video, several women interviewed on the street tell of their continuing struggle for equal rights at home and work. One in particular struck a chord with me, when a woman mayor says, "If I answer the phone, they say, 'Isn't anyone there?' 'I'm here,' I say. But if a man answered, they would never say that." My heart went out to her, for her story reminded me of times when I was a WAC in California during the war and answered the phone, "Lieutenant Johnson," only to hear dead silence on the other end until the inevitable male caller recovered from his shock at hearing a woman's voice.

Conditions for women in most places are better now than they were fifty years ago, but in both Japan and the United States there is still much need for improvement. No matter in what country we live and how much our living conditions vary, women around the world face similar challenges. Sharing our stories, our successes, and our continuing struggles helps strengthen us all.

Glossary · · ·

BCOF, British Commonwealth Occupation Force

BOQ, bachelor officers' quarters

buraku, subdivision of a village

burakumin, people of a special section, outcasts

chu, obligation to the emperor

CI&E, Civil Information and Education (a division of the Allied military government)

CPH, citizens' public hall

Diet, legislature

fujinkai, women's organization composed primarily of housewives

giri, obligation repaid with exactness

gun, a political division comparable to a U.S. county

haha no kai, mothers' club

headman, mayor

kabuki, traditional popular drama

ko, voluntary cooperative organization

minsei-iin, social welfare organization

mompe, baggy trousers for women

MP, military police

nisei, person born in America to Japanese parents

no, classical drama

obachama, aunt

obi, wide sash worn with kimono

oi!, you!

oludo missu, old maid

prefecture, a political division comparable to a U.S. state

PTA, parent-teacher association

PX, post exchange

SCAP, Supreme Commander for the Allied Powers; term also refers to the headquarters

seinendan, youth association

sengen, declaration

tatami, straw floor mat

WAAC, Women's Army Auxiliary Corps

WAC, Women's Army Corps

W&MB, Women's and Minors' Bureau, a division of the Labor Ministry in the Japanese government

Sources • • •

The primary source for this book is the collection of ten note-books in which I kept a journal of my experiences from July 1946 until February 1951. All quoted material in the book not attributed to another source is from this journal. In some places, quotations from the journal have been edited to make their style consistent with the rest of the book. Words in parentheses in those quotes are part of the original journal. Brackets enclose additions that the editor or I thought necessary for clarification.

Japanese and Americans are identified by given names first and then surnames. Pseudonyms are used in some cases. Courtesy titles (Mr., Mrs., Miss) are used with Japanese names to indicate the individual's gender and in deference to Japanese standards of politeness.

At their first use, abbreviations are written out, and Japanese words that may be unfamiliar are translated into English. Those that appear two or more times also appear in the glossary. Diacritical marks are not used for Japanese words.

Sources consulted for general background on Japan, many of which I acquired and read while there, include:

Benedict, Ruth. *The Chrysanthemum and the Sword: Patterns of Japanese Culture.* Boston: Houghton Mifflin, 1946.

Chamberlain, Basil Hall. *Things Japanese.* Tokyo, 1898; London, 1905. Reprinted as *Japanese Things: Being Notes on Various Subjects Connected with Japan.* Tokyo: Tuttle, 1971.

Embree, John F. *Suye Mura: A Japanese Village.* Chicago: University of Chicago Press, 1939.

Ishimoto, Baroness Shidzué. *Facing Two Ways: The Story of My Life.* London: Cassell & Co., Ltd., 1935.

Sansom, G. B. *Japan: A Short Cultural History.* New York: D. Appleton-Century Co., 1931.

Sugimoto, Etsu Inagaki. *A Daughter of the Samurai.* Garden City, NY: Doubleday & Co., 1947.

Sources quoted or consulted specific to a particular chapter are:

CHAPTER 1. The quotation on p. 1 is from Edwin O. Reischauer, *Japan: The Story of a Nation* (New York: Alfred A. Knopf, Inc., 1970), pp. 218–219.

CHAPTER 3. The quotation on pp. 25–26 from the *Kojiki* is from Basil Hall Chamberlain, *Translation of "Ko-ji-ki" or "Records of Ancient Matters"* (Kobe: J. L. Thompson & Co., Ltd., 1932), 2nd ed., pp. 22–24. The excerpts from *Onna Daigaku* appearing on p. 27 are from L. Cranmer-Byng and S. A. Kapadia, eds., *Women and Wisdom of Japan* (London: John Murray, 1905), Wisdom of the East Series, pp. 34–45.

CHAPTER 4. For more on the British Commonwealth Occupation Force, see Peter Bates, *Japan and the British Commonwealth Occupation Force, 1946–52* (London: Brassey's [UK], 1993).

CHAPTER 5. The editorial quoted on pp. 61–63 appeared in the *Nippon Times* of November 13, 1947.

CHAPTER 8. The quotation about the Buddhist nun on p. 138 is from Mary R. Beard, *The Force of Women in Japanese History* (Washington: Public Affairs Press, 1953), p. 104.

EPILOGUE. For more on the *burakumin*, see George DeVos and Hiroshi Wagatsuma, *Japan's Invisible Race: Caste in Culture and Personality* (Berkeley: University of California Press, 1966); Sué Sumii, *The River with No Bridge,* Susan Wilkinson, transl. (Rutland, VT: Charles E. Tuttle Co., 1990); and Bruce S. Feiler, *Learning to Bow: Inside the Heart of Japan* (New York: Ticknor & Fields, 1991), pp. 238–248.

Index

Acknowledgments

Heartfelt thanks are extended to those in both the United States and Japan who assisted with this book.

Neale Baxter, colleague and good friend for many years, encouraged me to tell about my Japanese experiences, so others might better understand that country.

Annie (Mrs. Midori Bando Sakai), in 1947 my first interpreter, read the manuscript mailed to her in Japan. Because I was reluctant to have printed opinions unsupported by a woman in that country, this book would never have been published without her help.

Mr. Akinori Suzuki and Ms. Naomi Tsunoda of Documentary Workshop in Osaka assisted by Ms. Tracy Roberts in New York City produced the 1991 Japanese television documentary in which I appeared, "Women Called '*Oi!*' (you!): A Historical Look at Japanese Women."

Mr. Toshio Watanabe, Buraku Liberation Research Institute, helped me be more aware of the plight of the *burakumin* (the pariah class) during two weeks spent in Osaka in 1993. Miss Mahoro Minami and Mrs. Yuka Moriguchi Tsuchiya were interpreters.

Mr. Kazanori Oshima, director, invited me to appear in the 1995 television documentary "Miss Johnson's Dream: Postwar Reform and the Women of Awa" (old name for Tokushima), produced in Tokushima in conjunction with the Documentary Workshop. Jean Gordon Kocienda was its representative in the United States. Mrs. Noriko Watia Nakakubo and Mrs. Midori Bando Sakai, from Tokyo, interpreted. Mrs. Hiroko Kondo was most helpful to me; I was an old friend of her mother, no longer living. Sarah Davies, a young Englishwoman teaching in a nearby Japanese school, played the part of Miss Johnson of 1947 in the documentary.

Miss Yuka Moriguchi interviewed me when she was a graduate student at the University of Maryland. She used my book, *Senryo Nikki: Kusanone no Onna Tachi* (Occupation Journal: Women at the Grass Roots), printed in Japan in 1986, to prepare her master's thesis before she returned home and married Tak Tsuchiya. Her understanding as a Japanese woman is highly regarded by me, an American woman. In her foreword, she explains the places of Miss Ethel Weed at Supreme Command Allied Forces in Tokyo and women's affairs officers like me in the prefectures.

My fairy godmothers in the Washington Chapter of the Women's National Book Association have watched with interest the progress of this book.

Dawna Lee Jonté, Barbara Molony, Eric Lindquist, and Diane Ullius offered helpful comments on the manuscript.

I am particularly grateful to Lynn Page Whittaker, publisher, who saw possibilities in the manuscript. Her skillful winnowing of the wheat from the chaff resulted in this book. Full circle has now been reached from Annie's reading my story of the occupation to Lynn's published account of my part in that historic period. Both are happily accorded my deep appreciation.